CAREER DIARY™

OF A

PASTRY CHEF

Thirty days behind the scenes with a professional.

GARDNER'S CAREER DIARIES™

YUKO KITAZAWA

GARTH GARDNER COMPANY

GGC publishing

Washington DC, USA · London, UK

Garth Gardner Company
info@ggcinc.com
http://www.gogardner.com

ISBN-13: 978-1-58965-054-1

Library of Congress Cataloging-in-Publication Data

Kitazawa, Yuko.
 Career diary of a pastry chef / by Yuko Kitazawa.
    p. cm.

  ISBN-13: 978-1-58965-054-1

1. Kitazawa, Yuko--Diaries. 2. Cooks--Vocational guidance--United States. 3. Pastry industry--Vocational guidance--United States. I. Title.

 TX649.K58A3 2008

 641.5092--dc22

                                      2008036439

Printed in Canada

TABLE OF CONTENTS

ACKNOWLEDGMENTS

I would like to thank my mother, Yuki, for being an amazing cook and training our palates from a young age to be discerning and curious, and both my parents for supporting me always. I would like to thank Masato Suzuki, my first chef-mentor, who took me under his wing despite my lack of experience and showed me the ropes. I would also like to thank my family and friends for their continuous support and encouragement, and reminding me that life is too short to settle for "just O.K."

BIOGRAPHY

I was born in Nagoya, Japan, and moved to California at the age of eight with my parents and two brothers. We lived in a typical Orange County neighborhood, inside a gated community with a pool and an orange tree in our back yard. My father, a businessman, often entertained friends and clients at home. On these occasions my mother would cook a feast of a meal, featuring everything from Japanese seared beef and chirashi sushi to steamed Dungeness crab, purchased alive from the local Chinese market. Thanks to her efforts, we learned from an early age about what constitute good eating: fresh ingredients, colorful presentations, and ritualistic meals at the center of family life.

Even though I've always appreciated quality food and loved to eat, it wasn't until home economics class in middle school that I discovered the joy of cooking. Since then I snuck into the home kitchen every chance I got, to bake cookies, cakes and tarts, and put together easy casserole dishes. My mother, who is territorial when it comes to her kitchen, was not very happy with my clumsy presence in her space. Eventually, she saw that I was serious about learning the craft, and promised to let me attend culinary school (as long as I went to a "normal" college first).

After attending UC Berkeley, where I received a bachelor's degree in philosophy, I moved to Hyde Park, New York, to realize my dream of attending the Culinary Institute of

America. In 2002, I graduated after an externship at the Four Seasons Hotel in Chicago.

After that, I worked in upscale private catering and at various restaurants before landing a position as pastry sous chef at one of L.A.'s top fine-dining restaurants. My evolving style is Californian at heart, with some Japanese influences, utilizing fresh ingredients from the farmers market. My original dessert, "kabocha crumble pie," was featured on MetroMix. com, a nationwide online entertainment guide.

At about the same time, I began to write about food, which led to published articles in lifestyle magazines (local and national) and a book assignment. My published articles have included restaurant reviews, recipes, product labels, short stories and interviews with celebrity chefs such as Nancy Silverton and Anthony Bourdain.

I am fluent in English and Japanese and have lived in the San Francisco Bay area, Chicago and New York. I currently reside in Los Angeles, where I enjoy frequent hikes in Griffith Park, and have become a student of yoga.

CURRENT POSITION AND RESPONSIBILITIES

I create pastries for a popular fine-dining restaurant in Los Angeles. The term "pastry" traditionally refers to baked goods such as pies, tarts and cookies, but in restaurant talk it encompasses the whole department responsible for the development and creation of dessert items (not only those made with dough, but including ice cream, custards, etc.).

Though my major at culinary school was general culinary arts (with an emphasis on French cuisine), I took courses in pastries as well, and I've been an avid baker since junior high school. Something about the process of combining ten different ingredients and ending up with a completely different entity, delicious and aromatic, was pure magic to me.

My duties include production, development and plating of various dessert dishes. This restaurant prides itself on its gourmet doughnuts, fresh-fried to order, so one of my jobs is to come up with new flavors. This can be fun, as possibilities are limitless—there are six doughnuts on the menu every Wednesday, and each has a unique filling and a topping. One day I had extra cookie dough on hand, so I took a pea-sized piece and wrapped doughnut dough around it. The cookie dough doughnuts has become one of our most popular flavors.

At the beginning of each shift, I take inventory. I check to be sure that we have all the ice cream flavors needed for the night (all homemade). I check for all other dessert components, test their freshness, and make a list of what needs to be made before service.

Then I move into production. I might have ice cream to spin. I might make tart dough, a caramel sauce, or custard filling. I might assemble individual cakes and cut segments out of an orange for garnish. Each day is different, depending on what we've gone through the night before, and what's on the menu that night. At around 5 p.m., I begin to set up the station for service. I line up small containers filled with sauces, fillings and garnishes on the counter. I bake off cookies and tuiles. I heat up caramel sauces, so they're nice and fluid. Tools are assembled together in a bain-marie filled with hot water.

A few nights a week I stay on for service, or plating. I love the creative aspect of my job and the fact that no two days are the same.

RESUMÉ

EMPLOYMENT

University of California, Berkeley, CA
Bachelor of Arts, Philosophy 8/04

Culinary Institute of America, Hyde Park, NY
Associate of Occupational Studies, Culinary Arts 9/02
- Dean's List for Highest Academic Achievement
- Perfect attendance
- Merit Scholarship recipient

SUMMARY OF QUALIFICATIONS

- Fine dining experience
- Safety and sanitation (certified food manager)
- Recipe development
- High-volume experience
- Ability to multi-task
- Exceptional communication skills—oral/written
- Languages: English, Japanese, Spanish
- Knowledge of multi-cultural cuisines
- Solid foundation in French technique

WORK EXPERIENCE

Pastry Sous Chef, 10/06–Present, Los Angeles, CA
At a restaurant regarded as one of the top fine dining destinations in Los Angeles, serving market-driven, creative, Asian-inspired California cuisine. Recognized for "Best Desserts 2007" by CitySearch.com.

- Responsible for production and plating of all desserts, including cakes, tarts, cookies, ice cream, sorbet, mousses, sauces, brioche, buns, biscuits
- Menu development: create and execute weekly tasting menu dessert
- Weekly trips to farmer's market
- Train and supervise new pastry cooks
- Maintain cleanliness and organization of pastry station and equipment
- Original dessert (Kabocha Tart) featured on MetroMix.com Web site

Freelance Catering Chef, 9/05–10/06
Provided on-call culinary services to upscale catering companies serving corporate functions as well as small parties in private homes. (Below are examples; not a comprehensive list):
- Celebrity A La Carte, Inc.—Acted as team leader at an anniversary banquet event for a TV show serving 1000 guests. Ensured quality control and supervised staff.
- Bread & Wine—Produced hors d'oeuvres and buffet items for a celebrity birthday party
- Taste & Company—Assistant chef for an outdoor corporate luncheon serving 300
- Organized and taught customized cooking workshops in private homes

Lead Cook/Supervisor, 12/03–9/05
- Prepared main courses, salads, vegetables, grains, and desserts in accordance with clients' dietary needs

- Assisted head chef in menu planning and recipe development
- Took over production of all desserts
- Implemented system for packaging and labeling entrees with improved efficiency
- Trained new employees

PALM TREES LINE BEVERLY BOULEVARD.

Day 1 MARCH 28

PREDICTIONS

- *Constructive criticism of tasting menu dessert I made last Sunday*
- *Brainstorm new doughnut flavors*
- *Prepare for investors' 15-top dinner*

DIARY

It is an overcast Wednesday afternoon and I am sitting outside Susina Bakery on Beverly Boulevard, with the relentless L.A. traffic streaming by. Three blocks to the west, situated next to a designer furniture showroom and a women's clothing boutique is Restaurant G, where I have been working in the pastry department since last October. Mondays and Tuesdays are my days off, so this is the start of my workweek, and I often come here before the shift begins at 3 p.m. to refocus my thoughts toward work and anticipate what's ahead in terms of menu changes and special events.

Ten hours passed since I wrote the previous paragraph. Now I am home. It's one o'clock in the morning and, although I'm physically tired, my brain is wide awake. It's like this every night. I'm so "wired" from the constant adrenaline rush of my job that it's impossible to sleep for a couple of hours. But I don't mind it so much; I use this time to relax, listen to the mellow night beats of my favorite radio station (KCRW), read by candlelight (the overhead light above the pastry station is obnoxiously bright, so my eyes need a break) and, if I'm so inclined, write. Writing is my second passion after food, but I don't mean to digress.

It was a rather chaotic night in the kitchen, but I had a blast. Wednesdays are "doughnut nights," which Restaurant G is sort of famous for. We make two types of doughnuts—cake doughnuts for glazing and brioche doughnuts for filling. Every week we offer eight flavors all together: four filled and four glazed. Tonight's flavors included grapefruit campari, lychee caramel, and vanilla brulee. The doughnuts are served with a miniature scoop of ice cream, chosen from six different flavors and all prepared from scratch as well.

There are two of us working together in the pastry department. Albert, a career changer (from being a TV comedy writer) and a graduate of the Pasadena branch of Le Cordon Bleu, is head pastry chef. He begins production around 11 a.m. Production means preparing the various dessert components to be put together at service. I am involved in some production as well, but my main job is to oversee dinner service. Not all chefs would agree, but to me, this is the most exciting part.

At 3 p.m., I join him and immediately begin "spinning" ice cream, a process by which air is incorporated into frozen custard base. It's easy, thanks to the powerful (and expensive!) Paco Jet machine. Each one-quart chromium steel canister takes about four minutes for an initial spin (from frozen state), and two minutes if it has already been spun. The machine does its own thing. All I have to do is drop the canister into a plastic sleeve with a handle, lift it upward toward the blade (the blade is attached to a rod that moves up and down and spins through the frozen mass at an incredible speed), turn it clockwise to lock it in place, and press the start button. It makes a really loud whirling noise like a bunch of blenders in a smoothie shop. When it stops automatically, I press a small button to release excess air, unlock the sleeve, and remove the canister. The canister now contains soft, smooth ice cream ready to be spooned into "quenelles" (a football-like shape, fashioned out of soft foods with a special spoon and several flicks of the wrist).

While spinning ice cream, I'm usually working on something else. In this business, multi-tasking is as natural and necessary as breathing. Today I prepare hazelnut chocolate glaze, crème fraiche topping, and vanilla pastry cream.

Doughnut nights are a blessing and a curse. A blessing

BLACKBERRY SHORTCAKE WITH ROSEMARY CREAM.

because it breaks up the monotony of serving the same set of desserts every week (though we change the menu frequently according to what's fresh at the market), and also because we get to have fun inventing new flavors. A curse because it makes ordering complicated for the servers, and consequently executing the plates difficult for us.

Tonight this is especially problematic, because the computer system into which the waiters enter their orders fails to register the new doughnut names for the week. So the tickets come out with names of discontinued doughnuts from the week before, and the waiters have to crowd our station and write down manually the correct names of the doughnuts. There is space in the pastry kitchen (which is connected to the main kitchen) for no more than four bodies. At the peak of service (around 9 or 10 p.m. when guests order desserts) we have four or five tickets calling our attention at once, so you can imagine the chaos with us trying to fry, glaze, fill, and plate doughnuts with the waiters nudging in to correct their orders. It is difficult to read some of their hasty scribbles, too.

At the end of the night, though, everyone has had their fill of doughnuts, with no longer than a ten-minute wait (our average plate-up time is two minutes, which is fast considering the complexity of our desserts), and leave the restaurant with satisfied bellies.

As always, I am the last person in the kitchen to leave. The last table sits at 9:30 but doesn't order dessert until close to midnight. Then I wrap up and put away the various fillings and glazes, scrub the stainless steel surfaces clean with hot soapy water, turn the ovens (and the fryer, on Wednesdays) off, make a prep list for tomorrow, change out of my now very colorful white chef's coat, and finally clock out.

It takes about 15 minutes to drive home, thanks to the fact that, at this time of night, there is very little traffic. After a long night at work, I enjoy the lively but lonely, flashy but somewhat nostalgic night scenery of Sunset Boulevard.

LESSONS/PROBLEMS
On Sundays I work the pastry station alone and, if time allows, I create an original dessert for the following week's tasting menu. Last Sunday I made maple-macerated blackberry shortcakes accompanied by rosemary cream.

Today, Albert gave me feedback on the dessert. He suggested that instead of adding rosemary-infused simple syrup (simple syrup is, quite simply, sugar dissolved in an equal amount of water) to whipped cream, I should steep the rosemary directly in the cream, and then whip the cream. This results in a more prominent rosemary flavor. There was also a slightly bitter aftertaste to the biscuits, which serve as the base for the shortcakes. Next time I will try reducing the baking powder.

PREDICTIONS

- *Enjoy a mellow night with reservations in the 35-45 range*

DIARY

I got up at 8 a.m. this morning to drive my brother to the airport. He is going to Japan to visit friends and relatives and drink sake under the spectacular cherry blossoms. My usual wake-up time, after hitting the snooze button three times, is 11 a.m. I needed two cups of coffee to make myself alert enough to drive. It takes about two hours to get there from Los Feliz, where we both live in separate apartments.

I still have a few hours before work, so I meet with a friend for a humble lunch of soba noodles on Sawtelle Avenue. This neighborhood, near the intersection of the 405 and 10 freeways in West Los Angeles, is where I go whenever I crave authentic Japanese food. Much more vibrant than Downtown's Little Tokyo, here you can find casual eateries specializing in everything from yakitori to sushi, shabu shabu, teriyaki chicken wings, and ramen noodles. Also not to be missed is the infamous Beard Papa, a creampuff shop pumping out addictive little vanilla cream-filled pastries to order.

When I arrive at work at 3 p.m. I am in a happy mood. I check the clipboard to see if there are any new events booked for the night. Whenever there is a special party occupying the private dining room (usually for 10 people or

---

FOR KIDS OF ALL AGES.

more) and requesting specific desserts, our event manager (Kathy) prints out an event order form and brings it to us. This form shows the name of client, date and time of event, number of guests expected, any special requests, and a detailed menu describing all courses from appetizer to dessert. We are usually notified of these events at least a week in advance, but we do get quite a few last-minute requests.

Tonight, there is a 12-top (that's restaurant talk for a table seating 12 guests) requesting a choice between After School Special and Bruléed grapefruit. We anticipate that at least seven will order the popular After-School Special, so I bake off an extra half-sheet tray of chocolate chip cookies.

RASPBERRY FOAM, ANYONE?

The After-School Special was conceived when Nels asked Albert to create a cookie plate as a permanent fixture on the menu (it's an easy sell and perfect match for Nels' rich updated comfort food). But Albert wanted to make it a little more special, something that would remind people of their childhood and induce a sense of nostalgia. The components have changed over time according to our whim and availability of ingredients, but now it consists of five treats: chocolate chip cookies, mint ice cream sandwiched between soft and crumbly chocolate cookies, grapefruit-vanilla soda in a shot glass, marshmallow cubes on skewers (toasted to order with a blow torch) with chocolate fondue sauce, and a slice of chocolate jelly roll cake (reminiscent of Swiss rolls you might have slipped in the shopping basket when Mom wasn't looking).

The Bruléed grapefruit, on the other hand, is a little more unusual. It consists of three to four juicy segments of pink grapefruit covered in raw sugar and caramelized to a glossy brown with a blowtorch, and served over a piece of dark Valrhona chocolate ganache tart. This is served with a splash of pineapple peppercorn sauce, with sweet-salty fried cashew nuts scattered around it. As a pastry chef, it is important to challenge and amuse the guests' palates with contrasting flavor, texture and temperature profiles on each plate.

After reading the specifications for tonight's party and checking the overall number of reservations (42, an easy night, which means Albert won't have to stay to help me plate), I proceed with my preparations for the night. I spin ice cream (making sure there is an extra canister of mint ice cream for the party), bake sesame tuiles for the tangerine bread pudding and other cookies, heat up the sauces, cut and skewer marshmallows, and slice a log of jelly roll cake prepared a few days before and kept in the freezer. After break, I scrub down the stainless steel work surfaces and take out the necessary dessert components in small metal containers from the "low boy" (a refrigerated compartment beneath the work station), which are then placed in a line against the wall, leaving the front half of the station clean for plating.

Service proceeds without any problems. Unexpectedly, though, we sell an equal amount of the After-School Special and the Bruléed grapefruit. Perhaps the waiter in charge was savvy enough to entice the guests into ordering the more unusual selection. Plating 12 desserts at once can be a bit of a challenge, but Alex, a 20-year-old skateboarding enthusiast and fresh culinary grad working the salad station, comes over to help me.

I plan on going to bed early tonight (meaning before 2!). I sure could use a good night's sleep.

LESSONS/PROBLEMS
In the case of large parties, instead of letting the guests decide what's popular and preparing more of that particular dessert, it may be smarter to train the waiters to promote the less-popular dessert. This would more or less equalize the sale of both desserts and reduce the possibility of our running out of components for any one dessert.

THE CIA CAMPUS (PHOTO COURTESY OF THE CIA).

Day 3 APRIL 1

PREDICTIONS

- Bake off burger buns
- Write recommendation letter for Leah, who wants to apply to my alma mater
- New sous chef coming in to train with our soon-to-be ex-sous chef

DIARY

Today is one of those perfect early spring days. Bright warm sunshine and a light, invigorating breeze welcome me as I open the door and make me feel glad to live in Southern California. I don't want to go to work! I wish I could go for a walk on the beach instead.

But the restaurant needs me, and it is a nice thing to be needed. It's just that sometimes I want to have a lazy, aimless Sunday like everyone else.

Once I'm there, though, I'm content. I turn on the light, the fan and the ovens, set my cutting board in place with knives and spatulas of various sizes, line up buns on a baking sheet for an egg-wash treatment and a second proofing . . . and I'm in my element. I'm happy, and there's no other place I'd rather be.

Sundays are especially nice, because I have the station to myself. Not that I don't enjoy having Albert around, but at the end of a stressful workweek I look forward to working independently; there is no one telling me what to do, and no one to tell what to do. I get to lose myself in daydreams while spinning ice cream, relieved of the pressure to converse endlessly. And it's a good feeling to know that I am responsible for every single dessert that leaves the kitchen tonight, from start to finish.

There is another reason why Sunday shifts are cozy and pleasant: I get to bake burger buns! On Sundays, Nels features hamburgers on the menu (not your average Big Mac, mind you, but 16 dollar-size patties made of premium wagyu beef—some people consider this a sort of sacrilege, but that's a subject for another day) and the pastry department is in charge of making the buns. I love the feel of soft, supple dough in my hand, and the yeasty aroma of fresh bread baking in the oven.

The dough was mixed, proofed and shaped into 40 rolls yesterday morning by Albert. Proofing means to cover the bowl containing dough with plastic and place it in a warm area to activate the yeast. After two hours, the dough will rise to three times its original size. At this point, the dough is punched down, kneaded lightly to smooth out any inconsistencies, and divided into four-ounce chunks. The chunks are then shaped by hand into smooth, round buns, and stored in the refrigerator until ready to bake.

Today, my first job is to take out the buns from the walk-in refrigerator, place them two inches apart on large metal baking trays (referred to as "full sheets"), and brush over the top with egg wash (one whole egg plus one yolk). Then I sprinkle the top with black sesame seeds and *fleur de sel* (sea salt). The buns are covered and proofed again for two hours, and finally baked at 375 degrees for eight minutes. They are delicious right out of the oven, although the grill cook splits and toasts them before serving. I can't resist snacking on a hot bun with homemade strawberry jam left over from doughnut night.

I almost forgot to mention there is one other nice thing about Sundays. An intern named Leah, a wide-eyed high school senior, works the salad station. When many of my colleagues are jaded and tired, she is still fresh and hopeful. I see in her a little bit of myself when I was starting out. Ambitious, fearless and maybe a little naïve, I knocked on doors of the toughest kitchens in Manhattan, begging for an opportunity to volunteer once a week. The fact that I was small, female, and a minority in a testosterone-driven world did not hold me back, though I'm sure some of these veteran chefs snickered at my audacity.

During break Leah and I sit together and talk. She hopes to move to New York and attend my alma mater, the Culinary Institute of America, upon graduation from her posh high school in North Hollywood. Today I set aside time to write a letter recommending her to the CIA's admission committee, just as my dear friend and mentor Nanako had done for me seven years ago.

Because Nels is a well-known chef, culinary students (local and not-so-local) often come to him requesting an internship. For the most part, free labor (with a fresh attitude) is good for the business. I say "for the most part" because for every genuine student like Leah, there is some poor disillusioned soul who thinks a degree from a culinary school is going to make him the next Emeril or Mario. Humility is perhaps the most important quality an aspiring chef can have. While culinary school will certainly equip you with the fundamental skills, knowledge and techniques necessary to succeed in the field, it will not make you a chef. It takes many years of hard work, dedication and perseverance, not to mention long hours and low pay, before you can break out on your own.

So it turns out to be another nice Sunday. Of course I'd rather be shaking beach sand out of my sneakers than scrubbing Grand Marnier caramel sauce off my slip-resistant rubber clogs, but hey, life isn't always perfect.

LESSONS/PROBLEMS

Before changing the CO_2 cartridge of the soda siphon (containing grapefruit juice), I failed to check that the cap was tight. When I tightened the new cartridge in its socket, all the gas leaked out, making a crazy hissing noise and rendering the cartridge unusable. There were no more cartridges, so I resorted to asking the bartender for a glass of seltzer water and mixing it with an equal part of grapefruit juice to order.

PREDICTIONS
- *Doughnut night once again! Come up with new flavors*
- *Begin planning tasting menu for next week. Go through freezer to see if there are any components we can use*

DIARY
Well, this is not turning out to be just another doughnut night. It looks like big changes are about to happen in G's pastry department.

Pick up any book on career advice and it will tell you that the longer you stick with one employer, the better your credentials will look on your resume. Working for the same company for several years shows that you are loyal, dedicated and willing to stick it out through good times and bad.

This common wisdom does not apply with the same strength to the culinary professional. A chef is encouraged to study under as many different masters as possible before reaching the level of executive chef (and perhaps owner), or executive pastry chef. It takes years of discipline, grunt work and voluntary studies outside work (keeping up with current food trends, visiting farmers markets often, reading cookbooks) to arrive at a point where you can take the ideas gained from various experiences and integrate them into a style that is distinctively your own.

TIME TO FRY DOUGHNUTS!

Because of this pro-active approach many chefs take toward their careers, employee turnover is as rampant as burned fingers and swear words in the professional kitchen. Well, perhaps it also has to do with the fact that this profession attracts creative types and free-spirited idealists, who simply cannot sit in one place for too long before getting antsy to move on and discover new places and things.

So when Albert announces today, as soon as I arrive for my shift, that he will be leaving in two weeks, I'm a little surprised, but not shocked. Something about his demeanor in the past two weeks told me he was no longer happy working here, and I knew it was just a matter of time. One suspected reason was that his affinity for using strange-sounding chemicals to alter the natural form of ingredients (i.e., xanthan gum powder as a sauce thickener)—a trend

ALL DRESSED UP AND READY TO BE EATEN.

among modern "food-scientists" inspired by the creations of avante-garde superchef Ferran Adria—has not been favorably received by Nels. There have also been personality clashes that led to extended periods of diminished communication and a general negative vibe in the kitchen, which wasn't good for anyone. He is leaving to head the pastry department of a new restaurant in Santa Monica.

At first I feel a bit annoyed. Annoyed that he has kept this news from me until now; it must've been brewing on his back burner for weeks. Annoyed because his departure may have consequences for my job. Who will be his replacement, and what if I don't get along with that person? Should I interpret this as a sign for me to move on and find a new position elsewhere that's better paying, and perhaps allows for more creative freedom?

All these thoughts whirl around in my head as I get on with my pre-service prep. Unable to concentrate, I step outside to take a deep breath. The power of positive thinking cannot be overestimated. After a quick phone chat with a colleague, I realize that Albert's departure would bring new opportunities for me no matter what. It's up to me to make this transition a positive one.

The rest of the shift is a blur. It isn't an especially busy night, but Albert decides to leave early to join his wife for dinner, so I hustle around quite a bit fulfilling orders by myself. This can be especially challenging on a doughnut night, because I have to run to the fryer on the hot line to drop the doughnuts (while avoiding bumping into the other cooks also busy fulfilling their orders), run back to my station to decorate the plate with sauce and a dollop of crème fraiche, dash back to retrieve the doughnuts, and then come back to fill or glaze them and top off the plate with ice cream.

The highlight of the evening is when my friend and colleague, Mandy, comes in for dinner with a companion. There's nothing more satisfying than friends coming to visit and getting to personally deliver the desserts to their table. Swing the door open, step out of the kitchen, and you're in a completely different world.

In place of the constant assault of heat, banging pots and pans and flaring tempers, there is a civilized calm, dim lighting, and a nurturing bubble of people coming together to connect in the most basic way: by sharing a meal. For a place to be 40 hours a week I'd take the kitchen any time—

that's where my soul sings, but a quick trip to the dining room to see smiling customers is always a welcome respite.

LESSONS/PROBLEMS

I have a tendency to react with the heart, rather than my head, when confronted with challenging situations at work. This is counterproductive. I need to learn to rise above my emotions and analyze the situation rationally. There are positive and negative sides to everything.

SWEET, BITTER, OR BITTERSWEET?

Day 5 *APRIL 6*

PREDICTIONS
- *Nels will talk to me about anticipated changes in the pastry department*
- *Prep for two key lime meringue pies special-ordered by investors*

DIARY
It is 9:35 on Friday morning, and I am already out of bed. Voluntarily. Not because I am plagued by insomnia, as I have been chronically since making the mistake of majoring in philosophy at college, but because I wanted to.

Since I started my job at G, I've been sleeping in nearly every day until 11 a.m. That means an average of a good eight hours a night. I need it, especially because of the physically demanding nature of my job. Besides, staying up until the wee hours of the morning and facing daylight when the rest of L.A.'s working force is already caffeine-fueled has become a habit, and it makes me feel kind of special.

But as with everything, it's not all sunshine and blueberry muffins. My relationship with Han, whom I've been dating for a year, has been strained considerably. Not only because I work Friday, Saturday, and Sunday nights, but because even on my nights off I'm wide awake until 3 a.m. as though someone had permanently implanted habanero peppers in my olfactory tract. Han, who is self-employed but keeps a loose 9-6 schedule, cannot keep up with my late-night hyperactivity. By 11 p.m., he is tired and ready to retire for the night, like normal human beings. As a result, our free morning hours are sacrificed, because I can't get out of bed before 1 1a.m.

This difference in our work schedules has caused a lot of frustration. For a while he's been a good sport about it. Recently, though, frustration has grown into resentment and resentment into bouts of irrational anger. Hurtful words have been exchanged, calls ignored, and feelings inevitably hurt.

The body is an amazing thing. You can program it like a computer to create new habits. My goal is to re-set my internal clock by next Friday. I will wake up earlier by five-minute increments each day, so that at the end of seven days, my wake-up time will be 9 a.m. I want to make this a regular habit, not just for the sake of the relationship, but to

NIGHTLY STATION SET-UP.

maximize the use of my morning hours.

After yoga class (which has done an amazing job of relieving my lower back pain and makes me feel clearheaded) and an annoying $50 fine for parking in a street-sweeping area (I completely spaced out after a long night at work yesterday), I arrive at work. As anticipated, Nels calls me to his office for a short meeting.

He tells me that Marie, a bubbly, chatty girl who oversees pastries for B (G's more casual sister restaurant, a block west on the same street) will be replacing Albert in two weeks. Marie and Albert saw each other as rivals, because Marie had wanted his job when Nels hired him eight months ago.

She had been waiting for this moment, and pounced at the chance.

I met Marie once, at the employee Christmas party last year. She seemed nice. The picture Albert painted of her, naturally, was not the most appealing. He made her out to be a difficult person to deal with. When Nels told me the news, I didn't know what to think. I didn't want to be swayed by someone else's biased opinion of her. She seems nice enough, and I respect her professional achievements. I will have to see for myself. In fact, I have seen a special-occasion cake she had made and decorated for a guest at G, and it was absolutely beautiful.

Tonight is insanely busy. We have a number of large tables, which is typical for a Friday night. Albert works with me through service. More than one table asks for our ridiculously popular chocolate chip cookies by the dozen, which aren't even on the menu, so we ended up having to "86" the After-School Special, which includes the cookies as one of its components. "86-ing" an item is restaurant talk for canceling an item on the menu during service. We don't have to do this very often but, when we do, we feel guilty and the general manager is unhappy about it, because it's usually the most popular item on the menu that we have to ditch.

Before closing my station I chop four pounds of chocolate: two pounds of Valrhona 70 percent Grand Cru Guanaja, a dark blend of cocoa beans from South America, and two pounds of 64percent Grand Cru Manjari, made with beans from Madagascar. The former is fruity with notes of cherry, and the latter has an intensely bitter coffee flavor with a long finish. Albert will stir the chopped chocolate into a new batch of cookie dough tomorrow.

One of the restaurant's investors is bringing friends for a birthday celebration dinner Saturday night. He has requested two key lime pies for dessert. We were going to begin preparing them tonight but ran out of time. We'll just have to wing it tomorrow.

LESSONS/PROBLEMS

I burned a tray of cookies, not realizing that a waiter had already turned the oven temperature up to 400 degrees to warm bread for customers. This usually happens around 6 p.m., when the first customers arrive and I am done with my station setup. The waiter, for some reason, decided to do it half an hour earlier tonight. I don't blame him for the mistake, though; I should have checked the temperature before putting the cookies in the oven.

PREDICTIONS
- *Make key lime meringue pies for investors*
- *A busy night with several large tables in the book*

DIARY
I arrive at work an hour early today to make key lime meringue pies. Albert is not happy about the odd request, because home-style desserts aren't his shtick, so the job is delegated to me. I don't mind this at all.

I began baking at the age of 12 after making peanut butter cookies in a home economics class. I became obsessed with the transformation of sugar, butter, flour and eggs into a totally new entity that was delicious and more than the sum of its parts. It was pure magic. Today, it still is, although I am now more aware of the scientific reasons behind the transformation. Baking is an activity that brings me a sense of calm and peace in this hectic world.

Making key lime pies reminds me of those years. Simple desserts are sometimes the best. With a creaky old wooden rolling pin that belonged to Nels' grandmother, I roll out a hunk of cream cheese pie dough into two 12-inch circles. I drape each circle over a 10-inch pan with a removable bottom, pat it down, and trim the excess dough by pressing my thumb against the fluted edges. Then the crusts are blind-baked. Blind-baking means to pre-bake a pie or tart crust filled with beans (or some other dry weight) to prevent

KEY LIME PIE

the crust from puffing up too much. Next, I fill the cooled shells with a mixture of key lime juice, sweetened condensed milk, lime zest and egg yolks, and put them back in the oven. When the custard is set (this takes only about 15 minutes), I take them out of the oven, and let them cool while I prepare the meringue topping.

Meringue is heaven's gift to pastry chefs because of its versatility and ease of preparation. It can be plain and white or flavored with chocolate, fruit puree, or various spices. It can be piped into individual cookies or used as a topping for tarts and pies.

For the key lime pies I prepare the simplest of meringues, made from egg whites and sugar and nothing else. First the whites and sugar are whisked together lightly in a

SERVE IT UP!

bowl. Then the bowl is set over a pot of simmering water and the mixture is whipped until hot to the touch. At this point the mixture is foamy but still transparent, and it has not increased much in volume. It is then transferred into the bowl of an electric mixer (Kitchen Aid is the standard brand in many professional kitchens), and whipped until the bottom of the bowl is cool. Now, the egg whites have transformed into shiny white fluff that forms pointy peaks when the whisk is lifted.

Finally, using a rubber spatula, I scrape the meringue into a pastry bag (fitted with a star tip) and pipe rosettes on top of the pies, covering the entire surface. Then I give the meringue a toasty makeover with a blast of our industrial-strength blowtorch.

The pies came out pretty—I make an extra one for a staff meal, just to be sure that they taste as decent as they look (and, of course, brownie points never hurt, either). My coworkers give a thumbs-up.

Leaving Pie Land, I get on with my pre-service prep. Since Albert is leaving, I'm making a point to learn one new thing from him every night. Tonight he teaches me his method for mint ice cream. Fresh mint is steeped in hot milk, which is then thickened with egg yolks and sugar. Additional mint (blanched for maximum green color) is added for intense flavor just before spinning the ice cream.

The rest of the night is well paced and manageable until around 11 p.m., when the investor's table is ready for the pies. Then I am forced to hustle a bit, because on top of taking care of the long stream of tickets coming in, I have to quickly decorate the pies (with candles and flowers—sort of tacky, but they requested this) and, after the waitress presents them to the table, slice them into individual portions.

Cutting pie is easy as…well, pie. But to make the pieces look extra nice, it is crucial to dip the knife (which must be very sharp) in a bain-marie filled with hot water between cuts, and wipe it clean on a towel. This takes a tiny bit of extra effort, but the cleaner, professional-looking results are obvious.

Tomorrow we are already anticipating 50 guests (which is a lot for a Sunday, and especially because I work alone). I plan to wake up early to drop off some books at the library, work out at the gym, and meet my friend Mandy for tea before work.

LESSONS/PROBLEMS

Since the key lime pies were a last-minute request, we didn't have time to find fresh key limes. We settled for bottled lime juice recommended by one of our purveyors. We were in for a surprise. When the bottles arrived, the labels read, "Key West Lime Juice" and, in smaller letters, "from concentrate." The pie tasted fine and no one suspected that we hadn't used freshly squeezed real key limes, but I felt a little ashamed.

PREDICTIONS

- *Come up with idea for next week's tasting menu*
- *Contact Marie at B to discuss scheduling*

DIARY

This morning, I had a hard time convincing myself to get out of bed. I feel lazy and my hamstrings hurt, probably because I've let too much time pass before going back to yoga class. But I'm determined to make a habit of it again, because the neck and shoulder areas that are vulnerable to tension build-up from hunching over a cutting board all the time now feel wonderful. The strenuous sequence of down-dogs and cobras, coupled with deliberate breathing, relieves stress like nothing else.

At 2 p.m., I meet my friend and confidant, Mandy, for tea at Susina Bakery. She works part-time doing pastries at B (under Marie's direction), and occasionally gives us a hand at G on busy nights. We meet like this every two weeks to catch up on our lives and get in on the rumor mill of the two intricately intertwined, drama-prone restaurants. Today I ask her what it's like to work with Marie. She tells me that Marie is generally an easy-going person but is set in her ways when it comes to techniques, and she does not like to be told she is wrong, even when she obviously is. Mandy also clues me in on other restaurant pastry departments that might be hiring. I tell her I'm going to stick around to see how things go. I can always change my mind later; I don't want to make any hasty decisions right now.

The first thing I notice when I get to work today is that the commercial freezer box containing all our ice cream is facing the wrong way. The custodian that comes every Sunday morning to deep clean our station has made a mistake. The front side with the temperature control dial is flush against the wall. To wheel it out of the small gap between the work counter and reach-in refrigerator, I must first remove the thick rubber mat lining the floor. Picking up the mat and moving it across the floor is like dragging a corpse (not that I've ever dragged a corpse before, but I can imagine what it might be like); it is surprisingly heavy and flimsy. Already sweating, I clamp my hands onto the edge of the freezer, shift my weight onto my heels, and pull really hard. The freezer is about four feet high and weighs 200 pounds. It's nothing to whine about, but I'm not exactly the kitchen's heavyweight champ at 5'2 and 100 pounds. The sous chef, amused by my not-so-graceful efforts, promises to talk to the custodian so this doesn't happen again.

It is a typical Sunday. Mellow for the most part, with a two or three frantic periods of many orders pouring in at once. One table orders all six desserts on the menu. It may not sound like much, but considering the fact that I work alone on Sundays, and that Albert's desserts are rather complex, it takes a bit of planning and thinking on my feet. Everything has to go out as soon as possible, and at once—not one plate can stagger two minutes after the others.

When I get a ticket like this, there is a specific sequence by which I deal with the different components to maximize efficiency and quality of the plated desserts. First I think of what needs to go into the oven: bread pudding, which has been pre-soaked in custard and par-baked, and two chocolate chip cookies. I put these on a sheet tray, slide the tray into the oven, and set the timer for four minutes. Now, I drizzle my sauces on the plates, and put down anything that can sit for a few minutes without melting, getting cold, or losing vitality. Panna cotta is unmolded and buttercream is piped onto a piece of chocolate cake. Finally I put down the more time-sensitive items (such as grapefruit soda poured from a siphon) and, by this time, the hot items are ready to be pulled out of the oven. I call for runners, finish the desserts with tiny scoops of ice cream, and off they go.

As I write this, there is an acute sting from an inflamed patch of skin on my right arm near the wrist. It's about the size of three pencil erasers. Towards the end of the shift, I reached into the speed rack for a sheet tray of cookies, not knowing that the one above it had just come out of the oven. The hot edge instantly singed my arm. Small accidents like this happen almost on a daily basis, so my reaction is one of quiet surrender, with maybe even a hint of macho pride.

If you want to know if a chef is really as seasoned or "bad-ass" as she claims, ask her to roll up her sleeves and extend her arms out to you. An experienced chef will have scars of various sizes and purple-to-brown hues scattered over his hands and arms, from the fingertips up to the elbows. And chefs are often proud of their "battle scars," eager to share stories about their origins. My own collection of scars is growing, much to the horror of my boyfriend; he says they make me look rather like a suicidal mental patient.

LESSONS/PROBLEMS

I need to be careful not to place hot sheet trays on the speed rack, especially in the waist-level section where frequent access is necessary during service.

DOUGHNUTS THAT ROCK.

Day 8 *APRIL 11*

PREDICTIONS
- *Prep glazes for doughnuts. Create new flavor?*
- *Go over any special events booked for next week*

DIARY
Ah, it's good old doughnut night again. This will be the last day Albert is working with me on doughnut night. Consequently, it's probably the last day for his pet doughnut, "The Elvis."

The Elvis is, of course, fashioned out of the rock-n-roll icon's purported favorite sandwich containing bananas, peanut butter, and bacon. Our version is perhaps even more delightfully artery-clogging: fried brioche dough filled with mashed bananas and peanut butter, dipped in powder sugar glaze, and topped with pig candy. Pig candy is roasted bacon flavored with maple syrup and crumbled into small bits. They are salty and sweet, with a smoky, meaty flavor.

If I were a customer, I don't know if I would be able to stomach an Elvis after one of Nels' very hearty entrees, but hey, novelty sells in Hollywood.

My own contribution to our over-the-top doughnut collection is the cookie dough doughnut. I figure if people are so crazy about our chocolate chip cookies and almost nearly crazy about our doughnuts, wouldn't they go manic over doughnuts filled with chocolate chip cookie dough?

Indeed, my theory grounded in fluffy-as-marshmallow logic turns out to be correct. My doughnut is a bestseller. I initially prep 15 of the dumpling-looking things by taking thumbnail-sized pieces of cookie dough and enveloping them in flattened brioche dough. During service I crank out a dozen more to meet the fantastic demands.

It is quite a busy night, with three big tables (two ten-tops and a nine-top), and a bunch of smaller tables in between ordering doughnuts non-stop. We total 92 guests, which is about fifty percent more than last Wednesday. We have been getting a lot of press coverage on our doughnuts, which might explain why.

I am also informed today of a special event on Saturday. It's essentially a buy-out (the restaurant will be closed to the public) and we are doing tray-passed desserts for 160 people, including 18 children. Tray-passed desserts are bite-sized confections passed around by servers to guests while they are sipping cocktails and socializing. They are usually much simpler and made in larger quantities than our plated desserts for dinner. The occasion is, oddly, a memorial for a deceased family member of the client. Hors d'oeuvres of miniature grilled truffled-cheese sandwiches and lobster bisque in shot glasses will precede the dessert.

So Saturday I will be starting early. I will probably go in around noon. The party begins at 12:30 p.m. and continues on until 3 p.m. We are serving miniature chocolate chip cookies (of course!), shots of assorted milkshakes, and flourless chocolate cakes garnished with raspberries. When serving a large crowd, we keep the menu as uncomplicated as possible.

The bulk of the prep for this event will be done tomorrow. Cookie dough will be made, rolled into thin logs and frozen, ice cream base for milkshakes will be made and frozen, and cake will be baked and frozen as well.

As far as my upcoming schedule change goes, Nels informs me that he will need me to work on the line as garde manger cook (responsible for salads and cold appetizers) one night a week. He is short-handed, because three of his line cooks left for other jobs within the last two months.

When I made the decision last year to resume work in the culinary field, my intention was to focus solely on pastries. However, particularly on nights I work alone, I often feel isolated from the rest of the kitchen. Doing garde manger once a week doesn't sound so bad. It will be nice to mingle with the other cooks and truly feel a part of the team. Besides, shucking a dozen oysters in two minutes can be fun sometimes.

LESSONS/PROBLEMS

I carelessly threw a Ziploc® bag filled with caramel glaze (made the week before, caramel has a long shelf life due to its high and practically pure sugar content) on top the oven to melt it. The hot surface burned a hole in the bag, causing an unattractive ooze of caramel to travel down the oven door and onto the floor. Fortunately the caramel is easy to re-make, but I was ashamed of the waste and mess I created. Next time, I will remove the caramel from the bag and reheat it in a bain marie over simmering water.

I faced another problem towards the end of service when one of the line cooks, while cleaning his station, turned off the fryer without realizing that I still had doughnuts to fry. It took me an extra ten minutes to fry three doughnuts because the oil had to be reheated. From now on, I will assume the responsibility of turning the fryer off every night.

PREDICTIONS

- *It is likely to be a slow night. Albert may go home before service*
- *Organize ice cream freezer*
- *Take ice cream inventory*

DIARY

Instead of the alarm clock, a fierce wind wakes me up, rattling my window. For a second I think it might be an earthquake. But the ground surely isn't shaking. It is a single blast from a wild windstorm that is sweeping Southern California today, bringing down power lines and even causing a brush fire in Beverly Hills.

Driving to work is a challenge. Commuters take their time to avoid palm tree fronds twirling and tumbling over the road. Two,fire engines wailing angry sirens, rush down Beverly Boulevard heading west, commanding the already timid drivers to pull over to the right. After I park, it is another challenge to walk from my car to the restaurant. Trash bins are overturned everywhere (Thursday is trash collection day in this neighborhood) and I have to dodge these while shielding my eyes and trudging against the impossible wind.

Not surprisingly, the restaurant is dead tonight. A small change in weather affects Los Angeles residents, spoiled by endless sunshine in a big way. A few blows of wind or a

MADELEINES.

light evening shower and they retreat into their shells like frightened turtles.

On Thursdays, I usually begin by organizing the ice cream freezer. Because we serve six flavors on doughnut nights, which are typically different from the ones offered with our plated desserts, I take stock of what's in the freezer and swap out whatever we don't need. Last night, one of the flavors we served was persimmon. Obviously, persimmons are no longer in season. Albert made a huge batch of persimmon jam in early winter, and a six-quart bucket filled with the pumpkin-colored concoction has been taking up precious space in the freezer ever since, so we decided to blend some of it into an unflavored ice cream base. Tonight I will not need this flavor, so I dip the bottom of the canister briefly

THE MIGHTY PACO-JET.

in hot water, run a small spatula around the edge, turn it upside down over a sheet of plastic wrap, and shake it until the chunk of ice cream falls out. This is wrapped, labeled with a Sharpie and stored in the main freezer for later use. I repeat the same procedure for several other flavors, and restock our little freezer box with flavors needed for tonight.

After the rest of my usual prep—baking off cookies and tuiles, whipping crème fraiche and heavy cream together, and setting up the station—I am left with two hours of idle time before service begins. So I decide to make madeleines just for fun. I've been dying to try the recipe from my favorite cookbook by Claudia Fleming, an amazing New York pastry chef. My roommate at the Culinary Institute gave me a signed copy after completing an internship with her.

I figure, if my madeleines turn out as gorgeous as they look in that glossy photo, I will make a batch for the memorial tomorrow.

First I melt about a quarter-pound of butter in a small saucepan and cook it until the milk solids caramelize and fall to the bottom, and the overall color of the butter is deep brown. There are very few things in life that are as lovely and alluring as the smell of browned butter. Then, in the Kitchen Aid mixer, I beat together egg yolks, brown sugar, granulated sugar, and honey (Claudia recommends chestnut honey, but I use buckwheat honey instead, lending the batter an earthy scent). I continue beating it until the mixture is light and foamy, about three minutes. Next I sift my dry ingredients (pastry flour, baking powder, and a pinch of salt) over the mixture and fold them in gently with a spatula. Finally I pour in the browned butter, whisking just until streaks of butter can no longer be seen, and the madeleine batter is done.

I take another glance at the cookbook for baking temperature, and am dismayed by the instruction to "store batter eight hours or overnight before baking." Eight hours! Half of the shift is over already. Of course, I can still test the batter tomorrow, and decide if the buttery little cakes are good enough for the party on Saturday… but I can't wait. Heck, what difference will a couple of hours make?

Well, it turns out, a couple of hours *can* make a big difference. Impatient and short on time, after just two hours I pipe half of the batter into fluted, flower-shaped molds and bake them in the oven at 400 degrees. Each cake slowly develops a knob in the middle resembling a camel's hump, a characteristic essential to classic madeleines. I'm relieved to see the humps. But as soon as I take a bite, I wish I had listened to Claudia. The wonderful butter-honey flavor is there, but my madeleines are on the dry side and too airy, not soft, dense and moist as they should be.

The problem is that I did not give the batter enough time to settle down. Whipping the eggs at the beginning creates a lot of tiny air bubbles. The batter still seemed full and spongy when I poured it into the molds and baked the first batch. When I checked the leftover batter after three hours, it had reduced in volume significantly and had the texture of fudgy brownie batter.

I will bake off the second half tomorrow—hopefully they will be as irresistible as Claudia promises us.

LESSONS/PROBLEMS
Have a little more patience and trust the cookbook author, especially if she is a James Beard Award-winning pastry chef. (James Beard Awards are considered the Oscars of the food industry.)

Day 10 *APRIL 15*

PREDICTIONS

- *An extended workday due to the special event*
- *Albert's last day; I hope we can make it a friendly one*

DIARY

I begin my shift at noon today to help Albert prepare for the party. I practically roll out of bed, splash cold water on my face, throw on a t-shirt and some crumpled jeans, and head out to work. Unfortunately, my grand plan to become a perky morning person by Friday has not come to fruition. No matter how hard I try, I'm unable to fall asleep before 3 a.m. I'm thinking of other possible things I can do to change this, like cutting back my caffeine consumption and practicing meditation before bed.

The menu for the special event consists of miniature chocolate chip cookies, milkshake shots, miniature doughnuts with two different glazes, and individual chocolate cakes with sweet vanilla cream. Simple, fun, kid-friendly. Oh, and with Albert's consent, I throw in my madeleines as a bonus… and yes, they do turn out irresistible thanks to the batter benefiting from a good night's rest.

My first task is to whip a quart of cream in the Hobart mixer with powdered sugar, vanilla bean paste, and a few drops of rum. I decide not to make it too sweet, because the cake is very sweet. On low speed I whip the cream to soft-medium

OUR "LIBRARY". JUST ASK CLAUDIA!

peaks, then scrape it into a piping bag fitted with a star tip. I pipe a small rosette of cream on top of each cake (baked in oval molds), and finish the cake with a single raspberry. This is an extremely simple presentation, certainly not something we would do for dinner service, but it is suited for a large, buffet-style party like this one.

Next I spin three canisters of honey ice cream for the milkshakes. Albert wants to use the honey flavor because we have so much of it, and we are no longer serving the Bruléed grapefruit dessert, of which honey ice cream is a part. Once the guests arrive, the milkshake will be blended and poured into shot glasses for waiters to pass around on trays.

Albert has already made the doughnuts, so the only thing left to do is to bake my Madeleines. I inspect the batter.

It is thicker and stickier than it was yesterday. This time, I pipe the batter into traditional madeleine molds that Albert brought for me. They are tiny and shaped like lovely seashells. The madeleines come out delicious, slightly crunchy and caramelized on the outside and satisfyingly buttery on the inside. An experiment borne out of boredom has yielded a valuable lesson: have patience and follow instructions!

During the event I step into the private dining room several times to deliver the plates of cookies. It is a strange atmosphere. Grim-faced adults, dressed mostly in black, are munching on truffled grilled cheese sandwiches and engaged in politely subdued conversation. Kids ranging from waddling toddlers to pierced adolescents are happily helping themselves to cookies and milkshakes. A European friend once pointed out that, in America, people often bash out in style as a way to "celebrate" the life of a beloved friend or family member who has just passed away. He finds this concept hard to understand, not just for the absurdly self-indulgent behavior and forced merriment of those who should be mourning, but because, in his words, "Why not celebrate the person's life when he or she is still alive?" I could not help but laugh and nod in agreement.

Anyway, the event is a success. Afterwards we all snack on leftover goat cheese tarts and bacon-wrapped scallops. Then I clean up my station, give it a good scrub-down, and start all over again.

There are 150 people in the book, but it doesn't feel that

busy. The tickets come through steadily with little idle time in between, but they are manageable. Tonight we also have the help of Nels' daughter, for whom the restaurant is named. She is a sweet 17-year-old girl who is aspiring to become a pastry chef. She comes and helps us out every now and then, lightening up the kitchen with her youthful energy.

The night progresses rather uneventfully. No unusual complaints or requests from customers (sometimes I enjoy these challenges). No petty fights with the waiters (these can be fun, too, to a degree). At a quarter past midnight we are finished. Albert says his goodbyes to everybody, trying not to make a big production of it. He and Nels, however, do not exchange a word. I wish him the best, and go home.

LESSONS/PROBLEMS
We overprepared (once again) for the memorial. A whole sheet-tray full of cake unfortunately ended up in the trash. Next time we will reduce the amount when there are other desserts on the list.

Day 11 *APRIL 16*

PREDICTIONS
- *Marie and Jennifer will be doing production for new menu*
- *Last day serving Albert's desserts*
- *A fairly slow night, at about 40 reservations*

DIARY
The ancient Greek philosopher Heraclitus of Ephesus (fifth century B.C.) said, "You cannot step into the same river twice." This quote suggests the transient nature of life; everything is always changing. Sometimes it is far easier to go with the flow than to fight against it or to try to change its direction. Sometimes you simply have to let go, allowing the tide of circumstances carry you where it will.

When I arrive at 3 p.m., the pastry station is a zoo. There are dirty tools, chocolate-stained rags, mixing bowls, and half-finished projects covering every inch of the stainless-steel counter, custard base overflowing in a pot and spilling over the induction range, and the Kitchen Aid mixer frantically whirling without supervision. The ovens are on but not at the correct temperature for baking buns, a Sunday tradition since G opened five years ago.

Marie and Jennifer, Marie's friend and part-time helper, are huddled in the corner over a pot of candied lemon, giggling and obviously enjoying themselves. They have been here since early morning to test recipes for the new menu debuting on Tuesday. They act surprised to see me, as

BRUSHING FLOUR OFF PUFF PASTRY DOUGH.

though they've forgotten that dinner service must proceed as usual and that someone has to do the prep. This is unnerving, because I've gotten used to the luxury of having the entire pastry kitchen to myself on Sundays. I enjoy the extra space, and the peace and quiet. Now there is no space for me to work on, and I am made to feel like an intruder.

It's true I'm in a cranky mood today to begin with, but this is too difficult. There is work to be done, as usual, but I can't focus. I step outside to take a deep breath. Alex follows me out the back door for a smoke. Noticing my distraught face, he asks me what's wrong. I tell him that the two catty girls have invaded my station and they are making *me* feel like an outsider. He coolly reminds me that this is just a transition, and transitions are always a little uncomfortable; the girls have nothing against me personally. In fact, they are helping me because, come Tuesday night, I will need the product of

ASSEMBLING GALETTES.

their labors. Marie is probably on edge because she is taking on new responsibilities and facing a tight deadline.

I thank Alex for the pep talk, wondering what sort of life experiences made him so sane, detached and rational at the tender age of 20. I go back into the kitchen and politely ask Jennifer to clear some space for me. They leave an hour later, realizing that I really do need to get on with my prep for the night. At 5 p.m., I bake off the buns, slice some roulades, and whip a batch of meringue with crushed pink peppercorn. I take a break and then finish setting up my station.

There are only 49 people in the book tonight, but it is quite busy. When I'm not plating, I'm doing some sort of production that Marie requested of me. One of these is puff pastry dough, which will be used to make apple galettes.

Puff pastry is a type of laminated dough, composed of many thin layers of dough with equally thin layers of butter in between. When you bake it the butter layers melt, creating "air pockets" between the crisp, leafy layers.

To make puff pastry, I first roll out the dough (which is similar to pie dough) into a large, thin rectangle using a wooden rolling pin. Then, a block of butter (pounded flat to resemble a paperback book) is placed diagonally on top of the dough. The four corners are folded over the butter block like a business envelope. After a rest, this "package" is rolled out again, turned 90 degrees, and folded into thirds. This roll-and-fold process is repeated three times (with at least an hour resting time in between to let the gluten relax). The dough is wrapped tightly and marked "I," "II," or "III," indicating the number of turns it has received. Today I'm able to complete two turns on four batches of dough.

In addition, I thinly slice about a dozen Meyer lemons. On Tuesday, Marie will simmer these in simple syrup to make candied lemon slices. They will be used as garnish for one of the new desserts. The Meyer lemon is sweeter and less acidic than the common lemon. You can eat the rind, too, because it's not overly bitter.

The last table lingers and finally order at midnight. I offer what's left of Albert's stock of desserts to the line cooks. They happily devour an assortment of cakes, cookies, and candied nuts.

I clean out the low-boy, reach-in refrigerator and the freezer, because Marie and I will need all the room we can get to stock up for the new desserts. I feel bad about throwing the old stuff away, but it's also liberating to clear out our space, inside and out, to make room for new possibilities.

LESSONS/PROBLEMS

I have to learn not to take everything so personally. Everyone has a job to do, and everyone gets stressed out at times. It's a waste of energy and time to brood over things I can't control.

PANNA COTTA WITH CANDIED
GRAPEFRUIT RIND.

Day 12 *APRIL 18*

PREDICTIONS
- *First doughnut night with Marie*
- *Visit Santa Monica Farmers Market*

DIARY
I just returned from a morning stroll at the farmers market at Santa Monica's Third Street Promenade, which takes place every Wednesday. I got up at 8 and arrived there around 10. It was warm and sunny, and extremely windy. The market was already bustling and lively, with farmers hollering "free samples here!" and shoppers of all ages sauntering from stand to stand, turning over and examining the season's best offerings. Beautiful strawberries and fava beans catch my eye, so I take some home.

It is Wednesday, and doughnut night, once again. But tonight will be different. Albert's gone, and Marie insists on overhauling the menu with entirely new doughnut flavors. I am thinking about this while driving back to Hollywood.

I want to do something with *kuro goma*, Japanese black sesame seeds. Perhaps I will toast a handful and grind it into a paste. I will blend the paste into pastry cream, and pipe the black speckled cream into doughnuts. I got the inspiration when visiting a Japanese bakery in Lomita, famous for its giant black sesame cream puffs. I tried one 15 months ago and still think about it often. The slightly bitter edge of the sesame seeds contrasted beautifully against the sweet, vanilla-scented cream.

When I arrive at work, Marie is shaping doughnut "twists" to be rolled in cinnamon sugar. I am beginning to like her more and more. I expected her to be a difficult person to work with, after all the awkwardness on Sunday and, of course, due to the biased opinions I heard every day from her alleged archrival. But she really seems to be an honest, sensitive and fair person, as well as an extremely dedicated professional.

Marie has been here since 6 a.m. today, working out kinks in the new menu and preparing doughnuts. Before she finally calls it a day at 7 p.m., she shows me how to plate two of the new desserts, which will be offered along with the doughnuts tonight.

One of the new desserts is a beautiful panna cotta, served

in a deep bowl with grapefruit soup, slightly thickened with gelatin. We garnish it with sliced strawberries, bits of candied grapefruit rind, and microgreens (tiny colorful sprouts) for color.

The second dessert, called frozen lemon meringue, consists of frozen lemon parfait over cornmeal cake, topped with simple meringue and browned with a blowtorch to order. The candied lemon we made yesterday will garnish this dessert, along with fresh blueberries.

Our new desserts are simple and elegant, without a lot of fuss. As expected, almost every table orders doughnuts tonight. It is hectic. While discussing my new schedule last week with Marie, I expressed my concern about working alone on doughnut nights. She recruited the help of Laurie, a server at B (the casual offshoot down the street) who wants to experience "the other side" of the restaurant world, merely as a life experience. Laurie is fantastic. She is enthusiastic and helpful, asking pointed questions and moving quickly to get the doughnuts out of the kitchen.

When I worked with Albert, he completed most of our production work in the morning, leaving me with little else to do but plate during service (which was, in fact, all I could manage on busy weekends). There simply wasn't enough work to keep us both busy at all times. Now, in addition to the nightly desserts at G, Marie and I are responsible for making breakfast pastries and additional dessert items for B. So there is much more pressure on me to produce, not just merely plates, during service.

FROZEN LEMON MERINGUE.

To use the word "pressure" isn't entirely accurate, because I love being busy. Tonight, in the midst of a doughnut storm, I manage to make two quarts of peanut butter mousse, a pound of almond cream, apple filling for galettes, and slice two pints of strawberries (tiny, intensely fragrant jewels with the stems intact). About halfway through service, Laurie is comfortable frying, filling and plating doughnuts entirely on her own, so I let her do her thing and focus on production.

When I finally clock out at midnight, the only other person left in the restaurant is the general manager. Even the dishwashers have gone home already. It's a little lonesome walking to my car by myself in the dead of the night, but I haven't felt this content in a long time.

LESSONS/PROBLEMS

When Laurie is plating an "All Eight," we notice that two doughnuts (Marie's carrot cake and my cookie dough) are slightly underdone, still doughy in the center. All the doughnuts are tossed in the frying basket at once, so it seems the two flavors require a longer frying time. For future orders, I ask her to drop the two first and wait three minutes before adding the rest.

PREDICTION

• *Prep for new dessert menu!*

DIARY

A rainy day. Everything seems slower, calmer, and more pleasant when it's raining. The urgency of everyday life splatters away with raindrops as they hit the concrete sidewalk.

It's 10 a.m. Friday morning and I am sitting in a plush, comfy chair at my favorite coffee shop on Vermont Avenue. I come here to write, when I feel too cramped and uninspired in my tiny little shoebox of an apartment to do anything creative. Last night had been one of those nights, so here I am making up for it.

Thursday night is my first full night working with Marie. It is also the first night we are featuring our new dessert menu in all its glory. (On doughnut night there are only two items offered from the menu). As hard as we have been working the past couple of days, we're not exactly ready, and we are about to get our butts kicked.

Marie begins her shift at 6 a.m. We are still at the stage where we are testing and adjusting several different recipes for each dessert to see which works best. Much of her time is spent improving the small amount of food we have prepared, instead of stocking up for the busy weekend ahead.

When I arrive at 3 p.m., it looks like a bomb exploded in the pastry kitchen—half-beaten chocolate buttercream smeared on the counter, candied lemons boiling over on the induction burner, dirty bowls and pans with scorched cream stacked high, and Marie running around trying to do fifty things at once. I ask her how I can help. Letting out an exasperated sigh, she points to the prep sheet on the refrigerator. "So yeah, there it is, you can go ahead and get started on pre-service prep." I stare at it blankly.

All the desserts were plated and served on Tuesday for the first time, but it was my night off. And the chart isn't exactly self-explanatory. For example, next to "panna cotta" reads: panna cotta, grapefruit soup, macerated strawberries, candied grapefruit rind, microgreens.

There are a hundred questions to be asked, but she is consumed with a daunting number of tasks to be completed by 6 p.m., and I sympathize with her impossible situation. I keep my questions to a minimum and let my instincts guide the rest of the work. Any discrepancies will be corrected as we go.

Preparation for each dessert proceeds as follows:

Panna Cotta: I slice two pints of strawberries (these are beautiful and intensely fragrant, smallish in size with stems intact) and lightly toss them with sugar to macerate. These will be arranged on top of the panna cotta. Next, I check the

CHOCOLATE BOX

grapefruit soup for consistency. The soup contains gelatin as a thickener. It is a little bit too jiggly, so I thin it with fresh grapefruit juice. Then I chop the candied grapefruit rind into small pieces, which will be garnished on top of the strawberries. Finally, I take a case of microgreens (tiny sprouts that come in vibrant shades of green and purple, primarily used for garnish) from the main walk-in and put a handful in a small ramekin. One or two little sprouts will go on top of the strawberries for added color. The panna cotta was made by Marie in the morning, chilled in three different molds (we will determine which works best).

Peanut Butter Chocolate Box: The boxes were assembled by Marie—a square chocolate-peanut butter mousse cake enclosed by chocolate walls made from pate a glace, a stable but rather bland glazing chocolate. I check the accompanying orange reduction sauce for consistency. I place this on top of the oven to warm. Next I chop smoked almonds into tiny bits to sprinkle on the plate. I make sure we have bananas, which will be sliced and caramelized with a torch to order. Finally, I fill a sugar shaker with beet powder. This is virtually tasteless and strictly for color. It is shocking pink, Nels' final touch to the plate.

Butterscotch-Filled Doughnuts: Marie made a big batch of butterscotch cream in the morning. Using a rubber spatula, I scrape the cream into a plastic piping bag fitted with a straight tip. I check the brioche dough, which has been rolled and cut into circles. These will be fried, rolled in sugar, and filled with the cream. I retrieve two metal bowls, one to fill with sugar for rolling and the other to line with paper towel for draining the fried doughnuts. The accompanying sauce is ginger caramel—Marie made this also. I place this on top of the oven to warm. Finally I supreme three oranges. "Supreme" means to peel the rinds off a citrus fruit and then slice each segment out using a very sharp knife. The orange segments will garnish the plate.

Cookies and Milk: Using a small offset spatula I spread pecan tuile batter on a sheet tray, bake until golden, then smear orange buttercream between two pieces. I also bake large batches of chocolate chip cookies and Breton biscuits. The Breton biscuits are brushed with egg, scored in a cross-hatch fashion, and sprinkled with cinnamon sugar before baking. Lastly I taste the malted milk, adjust its flavors, and warm it in a small pot.

Frozen Lemon Merinue: Check freezer for ramekins filled with lemon mousse. Cut Marie's cornmeal cake with round

CANDIED MEYER LEMON

cutter of the same diameter as the ramekins. Take out blueberry jam. Make sauce by whisking a small amount of jam, lemon juice, and a little water. Take out candied lemon slices prepared last Sunday and warm them on top of the oven. Check cornmeal cake rounds. Make meringue and place in a piping bag fitted with a star tip.

After a quick break Marie demonstrates the assembly of each dessert, and then I am on my own to plate. Between 8 and 10, the printer spits out a seemingly endless stream of tickets. I'm a little clumsy in the beginning, trying to remember what goes on each plate, but soon I pick up the pace and get back into the groove. The tickets keep coming and coming, tapering off around 11, with the final table ordering at about midnight. We sell about 45 desserts in all.

It was a challenging and chaotic night, but we've survived. We feel good about our new menu—the presentation, the interesting flavors, the relative ease of preparation and plating. It will continue to evolve as we find better ways to do things, but we have a solid foundation to work with.

LESSONS/PROBLEMS

It's too much of a hassle to heat a scant cup of the malted milk for each order. I decide to heat a big batch and keep it in a bain marie, set over simmering water, so that it is warm and ready to be ladled into a cup at any time.

SLICING STRAWBERRIES.

Day 14 APRIL 20

PREDICTIONS
- *Plate sample desserts for server meeting*
- *Catch up on production for busy weekend*

DIARY

Long gone are the easy nights working with Albert. With him, there was a lot of time spent doing particularly nothing. Especially between 6 and 7 p.m., when the station set-up was done and guests were merely working on their appetizers. I killed time by hanging out at the salad station. My coworkers passed over small bites of food off their menu for me to taste: lobster risotto, scallop ceviche, grilled wild boar. In return I'd hand them miniature bowls of ice cream with cookies. As you can see, I really didn't mind this

WHAT'S COOKING ON THE SAVORY SIDE?

idle time at all but, of course, I'd rather stay busy learning something new pertaining to pastries if given the choice.

So, things are very different now. No more time for chitchat or free gourmet snacks. If there's a minute to spare, there's a job to do. I can be grating ginger or slicing apples or shaping cookie dough. If I have more than a few minutes, I can make brioche dough or peanut butter mousse. Stocking up is our goal tonight.

Another element adds to tonight's busyness. Every Thursday, Nels calls the servers into the private dining room for a demonstration and tasting of new dishes. Since the dessert menu had a complete overhaul, Nels asks us to present all five desserts at the meeting. I will be in charge of plating, with Marie in charge of explaining. This starts at 4:45 p.m. Our usual station set-up time is 6 p.m., but we are not informed of the meeting before 4, so we scramble to get everything ready. Cookies and galettes fly into the oven, meringue is whipped maniacally at full speed, sauces come out of the reach-in and are briefly heated inside the oven. Spoons and ice cream scoops are placed in a container, which I fill with hot water.

Next I wash, slice and macerate strawberries, and check grapefruit soup for proper consistency. I pour malted milk into a pot and put it on to simmer. Working together, we go from having nothing to having five attractively plated desserts in half an hour. This tells us that if we really hustle, it is possible to cut our station setup time by half. Marie runs to the dining room where the eager waiters gather around, ready to dig in with miniature tasting spoons.

A delicious staff meal afterwards puts us in a better mood. Tonight we have grilled pork chops, Japanese purple sweet potatoes (I've never seen these before; they are gorgeous), and roasted beet salad with almonds.

At 6 p.m., I give my station a thorough wipe-down, bake galettes and cookies, check the consistency of my sauces, and go into production. We serve our first dessert at 7:30, and from this point until 11 we are bombarded with tickets and in constant frantic motion. There is not a moment to relax or even to use the restroom! We run out of cookies at one point, so I bake another dozen of each flavor on the fly.

Marie and I are both tired at the end of the night, but

satisfied. We've made it through a rough night. After cleaning up the stormy aftermath, I spend another hour on production, making chocolate cake batter that Marie will need tomorrow. Even the dishwashers have gone home at this point. Besides me, the only ones left in the restaurant are the bartender and the general manager doing their closing duties.

LESSONS/PROBLEMS
Peanut butter mousse is poured into sheet trays to be chilled and layered with chocolate cake. Marie taught me a trick for easy removal of the mousse out of the tray: place the parchment paper rectangle slightly off-center on the tray so that there is a "lip" along one edge, which you can grab and lift when the mousse has been set.

PREDICTIONS

- *Work on new cookie to replace pecan lace*
- *Make burger bun dough*
- *Heavy prep for a busy night*

DIARY

One more day and I will finally have my weekend. It's been a trying week physically and mentally, but I'm proud of the progress I am making.

When I walk in, Marie is standing over the induction burner, stirring butterscotch cream with a wooden spoon. She is in a great mood today, looking forward to her Sunday off. This is our fifth day working together. I'm getting to know her better and learning that we have some offbeat things in common. We both graduated from UC Berkeley with degrees in liberal arts. We both love novels by Haruki Murakami and can quote the same lines from Woody Allen's "Love and Death." A perfectionist, she prefers to focus on a single task at a time and gets flustered by too much multi-tasking. I'm the same way.

Today we are changing one of the cookie varieties for cookies and milk. The pecan lace brittles glazed with orange buttercream are adorable and delicious, but too time-consuming. Also any extras left at the end of the night can't be frozen. We are replacing them with triple ginger cookies, containing ground ginger, fresh ginger juice, and crystallized

THE COOKIES ARE READY.

ginger. One advantage of the ginger dough is that it can be formed into little balls ahead of time and frozen, so that they're a snap to bake. The pecan lace dough had to be spread onto a baking pan into even circles just before baking.

To extract juice from ginger, I peel and grate it on a Microplane®, put the pulp on a piece of cheesecloth, twist it into a bag, and squeeze the juice out into a bowl. The crystallized ginger is chopped into small chunks the size of chocolate chips. Besides ground ginger, the recipe also calls for cinnamon and allspice. We skip the allspice, deciding it would make the cookie too "Christmassy." We want to keep it simple and pure.

IT'S NO SURPRISE: COMFORT SELLS.

Next I proceed to the blackberry compote, which accompanies the apple galette. This is made by simmering two pints of blackberries in a pot with a small amount of water, sugar and lemon juice. I let it simmer for about 20 minutes, until the berries release their juices and mix with the sugar to achieve a syrupy consistency. This time I add a teaspoon of lemon zest to brighten up the flavor.

At 5:30, we sit down for a dinner break. Tonight, our grill cook has put together fried rice with shredded pork shank, and a side of wild mushrooms and asparagus cooked with wine sauce, reduced to a point where the vegetables are sticky and almost candy-like. Although I prefer my vegetables undercooked and dressed simply with olive oil, this is strangely delicious and I go back for a second helping.

Returning to my station, I put my sauces up, bake cookies, slice berries, make meringue, check ice cream, and gather the necessary equipment for service.

Marie comes back from her break with a look of concern on her face. Nels' wife, the operations manager for both restaurants, has asked us to start preparing "morning-after pastries," an assortment of breakfast treats for guests to take home. This was a tradition at G until Albert came on board. Now she wants us to bring them back. This will be a challenge, as we are already overwhelmed and working overtime. She says we don't have to do it right away, but we should at least start thinking about it.

As expected, doughnuts are the reigning dessert of the night. Doughnuts, doughnuts, doughnuts. I will probably be haunted by doughnuts in my sleep. The final count is 23 orders—that's 69 doughnuts I fried, rolled in sugar, and filled with butterscotch cream. Honestly, I'm getting a little sick of them, but we wouldn't dare take doughnuts off the menu. After all, G is famous for our doughnuts, and Nels' idea is this: Why make our customers wait until Wednesday night for our best dessert? Let's offer them every night! I never thought I'd be frying doughnuts in a fine-dining Hollywood restaurant, but there is a certain charm and romance to it.

It's clear that when it comes to the sweet finale of a meal, people want something familiar and comforting. This is where Albert's style conflicted with that of Nels'. Albert wanted his offbeat ideas to be seen, heard, and tasted. His "fruit plate" featured sliced cantaloupes, processed in a vacuum-pack machine to "rearrange their molecular structure" and served with black olive foam. He did it simply because he could, and no one else had. But if a customer wants fruit, a customer probably wants fruit—in its natural form, pure and unadorned.

LESSONS/PROBLEMS
The butterscotch cream is too loose; whenever I try piping it into a doughnut, it drips all over the place. Perhaps it wasn't thickened properly after the addition of egg yolks? Maybe we should experiment with another recipe?

YEAST WORKING ITS MAGIC ON BRIOCHE DOUGH.

Day 16 *APRIL 22*

PREDICTIONS
- *Bake burger buns*
- *Make brioche dough and Breton cookie dough*
- *About 40 in the book; not a particularly busy night*

DIARY
A slow, slow night. It's 9 p.m., I'm finished with my production duties for the night, and only four desserts have been plated. It's raining outside. Everyone looks bored, even the dishwashers.

It's Marie's day off. She will have every Sunday off from now on. Jennifer won't be here anymore either; she was just helping out that one time. I realize I was fretting over nothing. Sunday will be my day again, a day for independent work and quiet reflection. But now, I've gotten so used to Marie's frantic presence that there is a certain emptiness here.

As usual, I start with burger buns. The dough was mixed, kneaded, and divided into individual buns yesterday. After kneading, the dough was placed in a bowl on top of a speed rack next to the hot ovens to facilitate fermentation. Fermentation occurs when yeast feeds on the complex starches in flour and sugar and converts them to simple sugar molecules. Carbon dioxide and alcohol are released as by-products, creating tiny holes responsible for the airy texture of bread.

The shaped buns are stored in the refrigerator overnight. This is to "retard" or slow down the fermentation process. Long, slow fermentation results in bread with a soft texture.

I notice right away that the buns are a little smaller and tougher today than usual. Yeast is a living organism, so you can't always predict its behavior, even under a controlled environment. I proof them for two hours to let the yeast grow some more, but when the buns come out of the oven they are less than spectacular—dense, flat, and lacking in that sweet, complex yeast flavor. I'm disappointed. Maybe the yeast wasn't fresh enough, or I didn't knead the dough long enough to allow the full development of gluten. I will need to read up on this.

Next up on my production list is brioche dough. Now that we are offering doughnuts not just on Wednesdays but every night (though only one flavor is offered), brioche dough needs to be made almost daily.

Brioche is also leavened by yeast. It contains a large amount of eggs and butter, so the resulting dough is very rich and yellow in color. First, crumbled fresh yeast is whisked together with milk and sugar in the Hobart bowl. A handful of bread flour is mixed together with this, and then the rest of the dry ingredients (more bread flour, all-purpose flour, salt) are placed on top to create a "blanket" under which the yeast awakens from dormancy. After about 10 minutes I add all the eggs (28 eggs to two kilograms of flour!) and begin kneading.

You can tell when the dough is ready by pinching off a small piece and stretching it apart with your fingers. If it doesn't break, but forms a webby, translucent "window" (hence, this is called the "windowpane test"), it is ready. I place the finished dough in a bowl, cover it with plastic, and place it near the oven to proof for two hours. After two hours, the dough has doubled in size and nearly overflowing. I punch it down and put it away in the walk-in. Marie will use it on Tuesday.

Finally, I will make Breton biscuit dough (one of three varieties of cookies on the cookies and milk dessert). I've never made this before, but the recipe is simple and straightforward. The ingredients are simple as well: butter (premium quality is called for), sugar, eggs, flour. The mixing

EXTRA DOUGH IS BAKED INTO LOAVES.

method is slightly different from that of the typical cookie dough. A typical cookie dough is made by first creaming butter and sugar together until the mixture is light and fluffy. Then the eggs and dry ingredients are added.

To make Breton dough, one egg and four additional egg yolks are first whipped together with sugar until the mixture is pale and doubled in size (this takes about three to four minutes). Then, softened butter cut into small pieces is added gradually, beating after each addition until the butter is incorporated. Finally, the dry ingredients (flour, baking soda and a pinch of salt) are sifted over the top and mixed until incorporated. The dough is chilled until firm, rolled out, and cut into circles. They can be frozen at this point.

The resulting biscuits are tender and crumbly, with a rich

fragrance of butter. They are slightly more difficult to make than drop cookies, but are well worth the effort.

It's past 10 p.m. now. Still no tickets, no sign of new life in the dining room. I will jot down some notes for next week's tasting menu, hang around until the restaurant's closing time (10:30), pack up, and call it a night.

LESSONS/PROBLEMS

The Breton cookie dough is extremely sticky because of its high butter content. I have a difficult time rolling it out. Marie shows me a trick: spray parchment paper with vegetable oil. Rub a handful of bread flour onto the surface to form a powdery layer. Now place the dough on top and begin rolling it out, being careful to lift it off the paper frequently with a metal scraper. This works like a charm.

Day 17 *APRIL 25*

PREDICTIONS

- Charity dinner event for "American Idol"; a buy-out for 50 people
- Prep doughnuts, bake off cookies, assemble and bake galettes

DIARY

Tonight the restaurant is hosting an exclusive dinner party for the producers and performers of the popular reality TV show, "American Idol." This is the culmination of a special two-day charity event called "Idol Gives Back," raising money for children living in extreme poverty in this country and in Africa. On the guest list, among others, are musicians Gwen Stefani and Pink, though we never know who will actually show up.

There are three choices for dessert: cookies and milk, apple almond galette, and of course, butterscotch doughnuts.

When I walk in at 3 p.m., Marie has already taken three pounds of cookie dough out of the freezer so it is soft and easy to divide into individual 1-1/2 ounce portions. I bake off 50 pieces each of chocolate chip, triple ginger, and Breton cookies. I check the reach-in to be sure we have enough malted milk. We're a little short, so I add a cup each of milk and half-and-half, adjusting the flavors with the addition of vanilla extract, sugar, and a pinch of salt.

THESE DOUGHNUTS COULD BE A LITTLE BIGGER.

Marie has already assembled and baked the galettes. They are beautiful. The puff pastry came out especially nice today tall and thick with golden layers. I prepare another batch of the blackberry compote by cooking blackberries with sugar, water and lemon juice on a low simmer. I spin a new canister of honey ice cream to accompany the galettes.

Brioche dough was made the day before and already cut into circles. I test-fry one doughnut. I'm glad I do, because it doesn't puff up properly. Before frying, the doughnut is the size of a silver dollar. After a few seconds in the deep fryer, it should quickly balloon to the size of a fist and, when the outside is browned, the inside should be airy with a light web of dough. But today the finished doughnut is small and dense, even by the time the color has turned a deep brown—there's little room inside for the butterscotch cream. Not good.

We suspect that the problem is caused by a particular block of yeast. The 80 grams Marie used for the brioche comes from the same block I used for burger buns over the weekend. The yeast is old and, while not spoiled, it has lost some of its leavening power.

Marie suggests that we try re-activating the yeast by putting the dough in a warm (325°F) oven for two to three minutes before frying them. This works well. The dough becomes soft and puffy and, a few moments after hitting the hot oil, expands quickly to twice its size. Because we will not have time to put individual orders of doughnuts (three per order) in the oven, we place the entire tray of brioche next to the oven until all the pieces are puffed up.

During break, Marie tells me that a volunteer will be joining us Friday night to help me plate. Janet is a former flight attendant who is interested in becoming a pastry chef. We've had many such requests lately. This can be good or bad. A good volunteer will have a sense of urgency, plus a good sense to determine when her help is needed and when she should stand out of the way. A bad volunteer will try to show off what he or she has learned in cooking school and interferes without respect for our time-tested principles and methods. We hope Janet will be a good one, especially since Fridays are busy and we can't afford to have some prima donna occupying our space.

The guests will arrive at 7 p.m. My station is ready and I still have a little time left for production. I decide to make cornmeal cake (which serves as the base for frozen lemon meringue) and blueberry jam (which will be dabbed on the cornmeal cake).

Cornmeal cake is one of the easiest (and tastiest—one of our salad cooks always comes begging for scraps) things we make here. Cream butter and sugar in the Hobart mixer until pale and light. Add cornmeal, flour, baking powder, eggs, and milk. Beat on high for three minutes, pour into a full sheet tray and bake. Once cooled, I will use a round cutter to cut out circles.

Blueberry jam is made by simmering blueberries with sugar, water, and a splash of lemon juice. The fruit will break down after about an hour and turn to thick liquid. The jam is pureed in a food processor for smoothness.

Sadly, only 24 people show up for the "American Idol" party. It is an unfortunate waste of money, time, food, and space. The entertainment business is full of people who are fickle and unpredictable. Since all the desserts go out to the tables at once, we do experience a short but intense rush. Well, at least we are set on our prep for three of the desserts tomorrow!

LESSONS/PROBLEMS
Although the "easy" cornmeal cake comes out great in terms of texture and taste, it is uneven in thickness. The fan

of the convection oven blew the batter toward the door, so the cake is slanted and significantly thicker on one end. This can be corrected by placing the baking sheet on the lowest shelf, where it will not receive the direct blow of the fan.

PREDICTIONS

* *Production-heavy shift. Plating will likely be light*

DIARY

It's going to be a hectic weekend.

They are building a giant cell phone tower on the rooftop of my apartment building, not more than 10 feet above my fifth-floor unit. The construction has been going on for four straight days now, shoving me awake at 7 o'clock in the morning with constant hammering, drilling and outrageous thumps of heavy metal objects coming down over my head, as if King Kong is dancing on the roof.

But the real concern is what the tower will do post-construction. It's going to emit radiation that's known to pose serious health risks (migranes, infertility in women, even some forms of cancer), especially if one is as close to the source as I will be. When I express my concern to the building manager, he offers me a vacant unit three floors below. I agree to move to the unit, although the rent would be a hundred dollars more because it is slightly larger.

At work today, my head is preoccupied with the move, and drowsy from a lack of sleep. Thankfully there are only 52 people in the reservation book tonight. Piece of cake. Marie leaves at 4 p.m.

ROLLING OUT BRIOCHE.

On my production list today: almond cream, shape doughnuts, butterscotch filling.

Almond cream is baked inside the galettes, along with apples sautéed in butter. To make almond cream, I blend together butter, almond paste, eggs, vanilla extract, and almond extract in a food processor until smooth. Then I add a small amount of flour, and pulse just until the flour disappears. The resulting cream is almost liquid at this point, but it will set up and harden in the refrigerator, so you can pinch off what you need with your fingers when assembling the galettes.

Next I take the brioche dough out of the walk-in, which has been fermenting slowly overnight. The texture of the dough is airy and webby, a little sticky. This means that the yeast has done its job.

On a floured surface I pat down a manageable amount of the brioche, sprinkle additional flour on top, and press down on it gently with a rolling pin. I move the pin back and forth over the dough, applying even pressure until the dough has been compressed to about 3/4-inch thick. Then, I shape it into small circles using a plastic cutter. The circles are placed on a full sheet tray lined with parchment paper and coated generously with flour to prevent sticking. The sheet tray is covered with plastic and stored in the reach-in until service.

Butterscotch filling: We are going to try a new recipe today. The one we've been using contains gelatin as the main thickener, but the resulting cream is too loose. When the cream is piped into a just-fried doughnut, it melts into liquid and runs out of the hole where the piping tip was inserted. This is messy and unappealing. We've tried increasing the amount of gelatin but, the heat of the doughnut turns the cream to soup.

Our new recipe for butterscotch filling is based on traditional pastry cream. Pastry cream is thickened with eggs and a small amount of cornstarch instead of gelatin, making it more stable under a higher temperature.

The first step is to caramelize brown sugar (we use a special kind of brown sugar called muscovado, which is unrefined and has a deep molasses flavor) by moistening it with water and heating it in a saucepan over medium heat while

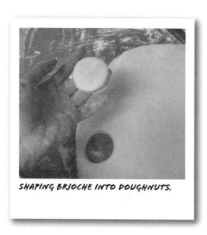

SHAPING BRIOCHE INTO DOUGHNUTS.

stirring. After about ten minutes, the melted sugar takes on a deep color and has a strong caramel smell. Now I deglaze this with heavy cream and stir until all of the sugar is incorporated. In a separate bowl I whisk together egg yolks, cornstarch, vanilla extract, and a pinch of sugar. To incorporate the egg yolks into the hot liquid mixture without curdling them, I first pour a little bit of the hot liquid into the yolks while whisking vigorously. This step, called tempering, is to gradually introduce the yolks to the warmer temperature. Lastly I pour the entire contents of the bowl back into the saucepan and stir until the mixture is thickened.

After break, I set up my station and taste the ice creams. When I get to a batch of honey ice cream made by Mandy last night, I know immediately what has gone wrong. It is flat and bland, lacking in that rich, creamy mouth feel. She's forgotten the eggs! So I empty the three canisters of honey ice cream into a pot, melt it all down, and add eighteen egg yolks (by tempering, as I've just explained above). I freeze it again and, at the end of the night, take it to the Paco Jet for a re-spin. It's much, much better.

This incident reminds me just how important eggs are in the pastry kitchen. They provide texture, form, flavor, and act as a thickening agent. They make cakes rise and are the foundation of luscious custards like flan and crème brulée. The most amazing part is that these are all secondary functions of the egg, discovered and developed over time by curious and hungry human beings! Primarily, eggs are just natural stages of the life cycle, symbols of fertility and new life.

Service is light and easy tonight, as expected. At 10:40 p.m., the last table orders dessert—doughnuts, of course. I wrap up, clean the station, remind the sous chef to order cream and bananas, and clock out.

LESSONS/PROBLEMS
Strawberries macerated the night before are somewhat disintegrating already and losing their bright, sunny color. Since they are naturally sweet and juicy this time of year, they don't need much added sugar. I will only add a small amount (to create a light glaze) just before service from now on.

ADDING CREAM TO GINGER CARAMEL.

Day 19 *APRIL 27*

PREDICTIONS
- *Janet will be shadowing me tonight*
- *Deliver chocolate cake and brownies to B*
- *Make ginger caramel with Marie*

DIARY
Work will be different today, with Janet volunteering for the night. She shows up a few minutes after 3 p.m. Marie has her slice a bowl full of lemons. While Janet is eager and confident, it is clear from the way she holds her knife (too far down the handle instead of choking up on the blade)

and her naïve questions ("What's a Hobart?" "Is the yolk the yellow part of the egg?") that she is really just starting out in the field. But that's all right. She is here to learn, and what matters is that she has drive. She has plenty of it.

While Marie supervises Janet, I take a brisk walk down to B to deliver a chocolate layer cake and four quarts of brown sugar ice cream. Nels wants us to do as much of the pastry production for B as possible in the G pastry kitchen from now on, because there is more room here and he does not want to hire a new pastry chef to replace Marie there. This is one reason my nights are a lot busier now. I'm no longer just plating during service; there is always something else to do. At times it's overwhelming, but I'd rather be busy than bored.

When I return, Marie gives me instructions on making ginger caramel sauce. We run out of this frequently because it goes with the doughnuts. Caramel sauce has many advantages. It's easy and cheap to make—all you need are sugar, cream, and a flavoring agent. It is also versatile. You can flavor it with a liqueur, or fruit juice that has been reduced to concentrate its flavor, or an essence such as vanilla or almond.

The first step is to extract juice from ginger. The hardest part of the task turns out to be, embarrassingly, choosing the right ingredient. The default ginger supply at this restaurant is young ginger, which has all the vigor and bright flavor of regular ginger but is slightly less bitter, making it an ideal flavoring agent for desserts. The skin of young ginger is brown and slick, not dry like regular ginger.

So I go to the main walk-in and seize the first brown, slick, ginger-like object I see. As soon as I begin to peel it, I notice something is off. First of all, the skin is as tough as leather. It is too tough to peel with a peeler, so I set the root down on a cutting board and shave off pieces of its skin with the broad end of my paring knife. The pulp inside is paper-dry and has a pleasant but dull scent, reminding me of the sandalwood incense I use at home.

Marie comes over and inspects this mysterious object in my hand. Neither of us is quite sure if this is indeed ginger, but I am having serious doubts. Embarrassed but curious, I hold the dry brown chunk in front of Alex, the young and enthusiastic salad cook, and mumble, "Um, what is this thing?" He proudly replies, "That's galangal. It's also called Thai ginger. We put it in the stock for the Thai lobster bisque."

Galangal. I've never heard of such a thing. How interesting! We are both humbled and happy, thinking about the possible uses of this earthy root in a future dessert. Galangal rice pudding? Galangal brown sugar ice cream, perhaps?

"Galangal, galangal!" Marie and I playfully repeat this word in a singsong mantra. Janet looks on, confused but smiling politely.

Now, back to the caramel. Alex brings me the correct ingredient. I peel the young ginger with little effort and squeeze its moist, intensely fragrant pulp through cheesecloth, collecting the juice in a bowl. Next I moisten about four cups of sugar in a pot with enough water to achieve a wet-sand texture. To prevent crystallization, I wet my thumb and run it around the inside of the pot above the wet sand. The sugar is cooked over medium heat until it caramelizes to a deep amber brown, then I add two cups of cream into the pot, being careful not to stand too close to the pot because the liquid will spit and splatter. Believe me, hot caramelized sugar is not something you want splattering on your skin. It burns and it sticks. Along with catching your knuckles on the blade of a mandolin slicer, it's one of the worst things that can happen to you in a kitchen.

The sugar will freeze up momentarily from the coldness of the cream, but will melt again as the cream heats up. The resulting sauce is a little bit looser than I want it to be, so I simmer it longer to evaporate some of the liquid. I stir in the hard-earned ginger juice at the very end. If you add it too soon, it will lose some of its vivid flavor.

The ginger caramel is a success. I don't regret confusing the mysterious root with ginger—now we both know what galangal looks like, and tastes like.

It's a busy night, with close to a hundred people in the book. I run around like a madwoman, composing plate after plate of endless desserts, struggling with collapsing chocolate boxes and under-proofed brioche dough, and teaching the basics of plating as much as I can to Janet. I am finished around midnight.

LESSONS/PROBLEMS

Wanting to learn more about ginger and galangal, I looked them up on Wikipedia. Ginger is commonly thought of as a root, but it is actually the rhizome of the monocotyledonous perennial plant Zingiber officinale. Cultivation of ginger originated in southern China and spread to India, Southeast Asia, West Africa, and the Caribbean. Galangal, or Thai ginger, also belongs to the Ziniberaceae family.

Day 20 *APRIL 28*

PREDICTIONS
- *Attend Festival of Books at UCLA*
- *Prepare for 15-top in PDR*
- *Make burger buns (with a few adjustments)*

DIARY

My morning hours are spent with Han inspecting books of all subjects under the sun on the lush, green UCLA campus. It's the annual Festival of Books, featuring over a hundred bookseller stalls, panels with well-known authors, book signings, and demonstrations scheduled throughout the day. We attend a panel covering controversial issues in food production and distribution from 10 to 11 a.m., then browse around. At 1:30 p.m., I leave for work.

The book festival proves to be a nice change of scenery. When I arrive at G I'm in a happy mood, even when Marie tells me there are 160 people in the reservation book! We've gone through most of our mise-en-place last night, so prep will be on the heavy side.

Among the 160 people is a party of 15 in the PDR (private dining room). Each guest will choose between two desserts: peanut butter chocolate box and apple galette. Up until now, Marie has taken on the complex and time-consuming task of constructing the chocolate boxes. It consists of a cubical piece of layered chocolate-peanut butter mousse cake surrounded by walls made from pate a glace, or glazing

CONSTRUCTING CHOCOLATE BOXES.

chocolate. Today she is going to teach me how to construct the boxes. I'm kind of excited.

First, pate a glace is melted down and spread thin over a sheet tray using an offset spatula. To smooth the top, I pick up one end of the tray and tap it on the table until the chocolate is spread evenly. The chocolate will solidify at room temperature in a few minutes. Then the chocolate is cut into squares, each side measuring 2.5 inches. The next step is to "glue" the squares together to form a box, using additional melted pate a glace. To do this, I take a square and dip the tip of one side in the melted pate a glace. I place the dipped end on the edge of another square lying flat on the table, at a 90-degree angle. The difficult part is to hold this steady with my hand while the chocolate sets. This takes about 15 seconds of intense concentration. I need a firm grip on the walls but not too firm, as the warmth of my hand will melt the chocolate.

Another wall is set perpendicularly to the first, and a final piece is set over the top. So what you end up with is actually a four-sided sheath. At service, this will be fitted over the cake, enclosing it like a gift. Initially we built the boxes by directly pressing the chocolate walls against the cake, but we found that the condensation from the cake softened the chocolate, making it dull and less appealing. By keeping the chocolate sheath separate from the cake (and at room temperature), its sharp form and appearance are maintained.

After a thorough demonstration by Marie, I begin to construct the sheaths. I manage to make four sheaths before it's time for a break. We have 14 all together now, which should get us through service tonight. It is likely that the orders for chocolate boxes and almond galette for the 15-top will be approximately even.

Next up are burger buns. Last week's buns were small and dense. I was not happy with them at all, and neither was the grill cook who toasts them off and slides a burger patty in between. Today I'm going to make them better by making a few modifications, based on suggestions by a few trusted colleagues and reading up on the subject.

I use half an ounce more of fresh yeast than the recipe calls for. After mixing the yeast with milk, vegetable oil

THE FINISHED PRODUCT.

and sugar, I put down half of the flour on top to create a
warm environment for the yeast to grow and let it sit for
10 minutes before adding the rest of the flour and mixing.
In addition, I make sure the dough is kneaded to the right
consistency by applying the windowpane test (described
earlier in the making of brioche dough). After kneading it
for about eight minutes, I pinch off a piece of dough and
stretch it apart. The dough is still too fragile at this point,
tearing apart without resistance. The gluten (a protein found
in flour which provides the elasticity in bread dough) has
not developed enough. I knead the dough for a little while
longer and apply the test again. The window is thin enough
to let light through, but sturdy and consistent. Beautiful.

Finally I scale out four-and-a-half ounces of dough for each bun, instead of four. I want to be certain that these will be bigger and softer than the last batch. I will not know for sure until tomorrow, but I already have a better feeling about these buns.

In the meantime, Marie is working on a birthday plate requested by a guest celebrating his wife's birthday. She melts a small amount of 66 percent Valrhona chocolate in a pan, pours it into a cornette (a small, cone-shaped bag made from parchment paper with a needlepin-size hole at the bottom), and uses this to write "Happy Birthday Luca" on the plate in pretty cursive letters. The plate will be kept in a dry place until the guests are ready for dessert.

I glance at the clock. It's already 6 p.m.—time has passed by quickly. I need to set up for service as quickly as possible. I whip up a batch of meringue, bake off cookies, check the ice creams for consistency (they are all fine, no need to re-spin), warm some malted milk, and thin the blueberry-lemon sauce with a little bit of water (the high pectin content makes it gloppy after sitting in the refrigerator overnight). I take out everything I need for service and place them on my station.

Service is hectic, but I manage with increased confidence. The doughnuts are giving me a bit of trouble again by not rising enough. I correct this by taking the entire sheet tray of dough out of the refrigerator and setting it aside next to the oven for half an hour to reactivate the yeast. The brioche pieces are puffy and airy now. The sheet tray goes back into the refrigerator, and pieces of dough will be taken out as needed and will go straight to the fryer. I find this procedure much more efficient than re-proofing each batch of doughnuts before frying, as we have done earlier this week.

I clock out at 1 a.m. It's been a long day. I will sleep well tonight.

LESSONS/PROBLEMS
The doughnuts should be cut and shaped as early as possible, to allow time for further proofing out of the refrigerator. Rolling the dough flat also causes it to shrink and tighten, so it is necessary to give it a few hours to relax afterwards.

PREDICTIONS

- *Make more chocolate boxes (went through all but three last night!)*
- *Make brioche dough*
- *Bake off buns*

DIARY

It is extraordinarily warm today, about 85 degrees outside. It's also warmer than usual inside the kitchen. This means that the construction of the heat-sensitive chocolate boxes will have to wait. The ones I made yesterday are kept in an airtight plastic box at the bar, where it is much cooler.

There is an upside to the warm temperature. The buns are rising quickly! The yeast will have no problem doing its job today. An hour after I bring them back to room temperature, the buns are nicely puffed up and ready to go into the oven. They turn out beautifully. Even crumbs, soft airy texture, a faintly sweet and eggy flavor.

At 6 p.m., I make brioche dough and while it's kneading, I do my usual station set-up: bake cookies, cut out cornmeal cake, make meringue, bake galettes, check ice cream, put sauces out.

I should mention that the meringue I make now is a different type from the one I made for the key lime pies, as well as Albert's version of lemon meringue tart. Albert preferred

BURGER BUNS: NEW AND IMPROVED!

Swiss meringue, which is made by whisking egg whites with sugar over simmering water, then beating the mixture with an electric mixer. Now I make Italian meringue, which is cooked to a higher temperature and therefore is more stable.

Italian meringue is made by pouring syrup (sugar boiled to 240 degrees) over beaten egg whites. The mixture will be beaten until the bottom of the bowl is cool to the touch. Egg whites will increase about six times their original volume. While Swiss meringue can deflate and begin to separate after a few hours, Italian meringue will hold its shape and usability for three days, if made properly.

For dinner we have spaghetti and meatballs. Sometimes, a simple home-style meal is what we crave the most. I sit with Leah, the CIA-bound intern, and Dan, a new guy on sauté. Dan had also gone to the CIA, so we reminisce over

MY SUNDAY BABIES.

our experiences and forewarn Leah about the militant fish butchery instructor who made all the girls cry on the first day. I was scared of him and, yes, he did make me cry once when he yelled at me for using the wrong container for breading cod fillets. But before the end of the three-week course he revealed himself to be a gentle soul beneath the tough exterior, and the entire class loved him.

Service is interrupted briefly when the printer stops working around 8 p.m. One of the waitresses comes to check on the progress of a dessert she ordered 20 minutes ago, but we don't have a ticket for it. I ask Jeremy to inspect the printer while I quickly plate the panna cotta. The connection of the printer cable to the wall jack had been loose. So he disconnects it plugs it back in again, and runs a print test. It's working again. Good. We haven't missed any other orders; thank God it's not a Friday night.

The rest of the night proceeds slowly but smoothly, without further problems. At 42 covers, it's not an especially busy night. There are about two-dozen buns left over and, since they turned out great, I freeze them in Ziploc® bags for the staff meal next week. I'm also able to get additional production done: Breton biscuit dough and vanilla ice cream base. At 10:45 p.m. I close my station, wrap up five yellow round cakes Marie baked for B, and go home.

LESSONS/PROBLEMS
The modified burger buns are a success. In summary, an increased amount of yeast, more activation time before mixing, and thorough development of gluten are key. I feel much more confident about making them.

PREDICTIONS

- Discuss tasting menu dessert with Marie
- Think about new chocolate dessert and accompanying ice cream
- Doughnut night once again. 56 in reservation book so far

DIARY

After a midday coffee break, I arrive at work. My first job today is to spin ice cream. There is a problem: the blade of the Paco Jet machine is missing! I tell Marie and we look everywhere. Then a thought hits me: "Hey Marie, did you work with Mandy yesterday?" Mandy is the part-time girl who comes to help us on an irregular basis. "Yeah, why?" Marie asks.

I dig through the ice cream freezer and find two flavors still contained in their canisters (others have been transferred into plastic containers). I pick the blueberry malt and, with a metal spatula, start breaking up the ice cream until I hit a metal object. Just what I thought! This has happened before, when I assigned Mandy to spin the ice cream. She must have had a rough night.

Here is what happened. Sometimes, when the canister is dislodged from the Paco Jet machine, the blade falls on top of the ice cream. If the ice cream is extremely soft, the blade sinks down. Of course the appropriate thing to do is to fish out the blade, clean it, and reattach it to the machine.

Mandy was probably distracted at the time and did not realize that the blade had sunk to the bottom of the canister. It happens.

After this unplanned excavation of the Paco Jet blade, I proceed to spin ice cream. Today we have a new flavor: Siam tea. This was Marie's idea and we are thinking of serving it with a new chocolate dessert. Siam tea has a distinctive, minty-herbal flavor that's subtle and refreshing. It complements the bittersweet taste of chocolate harmoniously.

My next job is to assemble blueberry brown butter tarts. Nels, our executive chef, has come up with a new concept for the weekly tasting menu called "Close To Home." The menu consists of four courses and a dessert made with ingredients that are grown locally. "Locally" is defined as within a 400-mile radius.

It is important to use local ingredients for several reasons. First, vegetables and fruits grown locally do not travel hundreds or thousands of miles to reach our dinner plates, so they are fresher and better tasting. Also, we are helping the environment by reducing problems associated with fossil fuel usage. The burning of fossil fuel is a major contributor to global warming and poses health risks to humans. Moreover, we are supporting sustainable farmers who have an interest in preserving the condition of surrounding lands, and who pay fair wages to their workers.

The tart dough is made with crushed almonds grown

HOLLYWOOD HOOPLA OUTSIDE MY APARTMENT.

in California. The filling consists of berries (blueberries, huckleberries and blackberries) purchased from the Santa Monica Farmers Market.

Marie made the dough in the morning. To assemble the dessert, I first roll out the dough with a wooden pin and cut it into circles about five inches in diameter. Then I fit the circles into ring molds, pressing the dough down and up the sides. These tart shells are filled with a mixture of brown butter, sugar and eggs, and topped with berries macerated in sugar for gloss and moisture. They are baked in the ring molds for about 25 minutes, until the tart shell is golden brown and the filling has puffed up. The tarts will be served with a dollop of crème fraiche on top.

Now on to doughnuts. We are using the same glazes and

BERRY TARTS MADE FROM LOCAL INGREDIENTS.

fillings as last week. The glazes contain so much sugar that they keep for weeks, so we are using the ones made last week and stored in Ziploc® bags. Marie has already shaped the doughnuts—cake doughnuts with holes for glazing, brioche rounds for filling, and twists for dusting with cinnamon sugar. All I have to do is empty the glazes into metal containers, fill pastry bags with various creams and strawberry jam, and wrap a dozen pieces of chocolate chip cookie dough with brioche. All this takes about half an hour.

Between 6 and 8 p.m., I keep myself busy with additional production work. I make a gallon of malted milk, some candied lemons, and orange juice reduction.

Around 8:30 p.m., the doughnut orders start coming, and between 9 and 10:30 I am completely swamped. The orange juice has reduced to an unpleasantly bitter syrup because I did not have a moment to check on it. "American Idol" judge Randy Jackson is here for doughnuts, wearing a jacket decorated with diamonds in the shape of a skull, according to a waiter. I want to take a peek, but there is no time.

At 11, all tables are cleared. I'd promised Alex, one of the line cooks, a S'mores doughnut, so I fry one off. He takes a contemplative bite and says, "Wow. It goes fluffy, fluffy, then goo," describing the textures of the meringue topping (fluffy), the brioche (fluffy), and the chocolate pastry cream inside (goo). It's been a hectic night, but at least I made someone happy. Time to go home.

LESSONS/PROBLEMS
I need to learn my limits and not take on too much production during service. Besides over-reducing orange juice, I also dumped about a quart of the malted milk on the floor while trying to transfer it into a container, in a hectic haze. Maybe I'm just a little clumsy today, but I probably need to slow down a bit so as not to compromise the quality of my work.

PREDICTIONS

- *Assemble galettes for party on Saturday*
- *Make lemon parfait filling*
- *Introduce new chocolate dessert?*

DIARY

I get to work and Marie has tallied up the doughnut sales from last night by going through the big pile of tickets I'd left on the spindle. Predictably, the best-selling flavors are those that make our customers feel like kids again. First place is a tie between S'mores and peanut butter-chocolate. At second place is chocolate chip cookie dough, then following close behind, chocolate covered strawberry.

S'mores doughnuts consist of chocolate pastry cream filling and "campfire marshmallow" on top, which is actually piped meringue toasted with a blowtorch. Peanut butter-chocolate is simply a sweet peanut butter frosted doughnut with dark chocolate drizzled on top. Chocolate chip cookie dough is made by wrapping flattened brioche around a pea-sized piece of cookie dough, then frying it until the outside is brown and the inside is a chocolaty, oozy mess. And finally, chocolate-covered strawberry features brioche filled with homemade strawberry jam, rolled in sugar, and drizzled with chocolate. Needless to say, each of the top four flavors has chocolate in some form.

Among the less popular are Meyer lemon glaze and carrot cake. These are flavors Marie worked the hardest on, with an intention to offer something a little offbeat and interesting. I guess it doesn't take a lot to please people when it comes to doughnuts.

Today on my production list are lemon parfait filling (which serves as the base for frozen lemon meringue), and the assembly of apple galettes.

The word "parfait" conjures up images of tall glasses filled with colorful layers of ice cream, fruit, and mousse, topped off with a squirt of Reddi-Wip™ and chopped nuts. However, in the world of French pastries, parfait (meaning "perfect") is a much simpler dessert: a frozen custard made with egg yolks, sugar, and a flavoring agent, set in a mold. Because it is not aerated like ice cream, parfait is richer and denser in texture.

To make lemon parfait, I whip egg yolks and sugar together in the Kitchen Aid mixer to ribbon stage. At the same time, I boil sugar and water to 240 degrees, and pour it in a thin stream into the eggs (when they have reached ribbon stage). I continue to whip this until the bottom of the bowl feels cool to the touch. Finally I whisk in lemon juice and fold in softly whipped cream. This light, airy mixture is poured into individual molds and frozen.

Stephanie, our new events manager, informs us that there will be a special event for lunch on Saturday. Marie will be overseeing service, but I am helping her prepare apple

BOILING SUGAR FOR LEMON PARFAIT.

galettes, one of the dessert choices for the 50 guests scheduled to attend.

Marie shows me after break and station setup how the galettes are assembled. Two puff pastry circles, about four inches in diameter and made several days before, are taken out of the freezer to thaw. When they are reasonably pliable, I place a mound of almond cream in the middle of one circle and cover it with sliced sautéed apples. Then I score the top of the second circle with a sharp paring knife in the shape of a daisy and brush over the top and around the edge of the first circle with egg wash. Next I drape the scored circle over the other, sealing the edges together. This is frozen again until it is ready to be baked. Whenever I have a moment between plating desserts, I soften the puff pastry by pressing

WHIPPING EGG BASE FOR LEMON PARFAIT.

it between my palms, sending pleasant waves of coldness through my wrists and up to my elbows.

Tonight we are introducing a new chocolate dessert. No, we're not kicking the peanut butter chocolate box off the menu yet, though they are a pain to make. Nels insists one chocolate dessert on the menu isn't enough. The doughnut tally convinces me he is right.

The new dessert, entirely conceived by Marie, consists of Boca Negra (a very thick, pudding-like chocolate cake) on a flattened circular piece of curried Rice Krispie treat, Siam tea ice cream, and passion fruit caramel. The combination of flavors, as weird as it might sound, works beautifully.

During service, Marie and I are in a silly mood, probably due to overcaffeination. While she stirs coffee ice cream base and I rearrange my mise-en-place for the fifth time because we are not getting any tickets (though it does get a bit busy later), we compete to see who can remember the cheesiest song from the '80s. We get a little carried away with this; an hour later, all the cooks are burdened with a certain Tears For Fears song stuck in their heads.

The campy atmosphere does not last long, as it turns out to be a hectic night. According to the reservation report we only have 46 guests tonight, but this isn't the whole picture, because we also accommodate walk-ins whenever possible.

The last table to order, around 10:30, is a seven-top and the biggest table of the night. They have three orders of doughnuts and a galette. How anti-climatic. After putting everything away and scrubbing my station, there are still a few things left to do. Coffee ice cream base made by Marie—about two gallons of it!—is sitting in an ice bath. I need to pour the base into canisters (which we might not have enough of that are empty, which means I'd have to unmold already frozen ones, wrap and label those, too), cover and label them, and put them away in the freezer. It's one of those tedious things you can't avoid doing, like laundry. There are also six pans of sponge cake in the oven, which must be taken out in 15 minutes, cooled down, and put away. At 11:45 p.m. I am finally finished.

LESSONS/PROBLEMS

The chocolate in Boca Negra is so intense that it overwhelms the curry in the Rice Krispy Treat. We adjust this by adding a teaspoon of sweet Madras curry (which is more complex and powerful than the generic curry we initially used). Now the two flavors balance each other.

Day 24 *MAY 4*

PREDICTIONS
- *Bar Mitzvah event*
- *Make burger buns*
- *Show Marie how to make sugared pistachios*

DIARY

I get to work at 3 p.m. as usual. It's not a pretty sight. Marie is shuffling several sheet trays of cookies in and out of the oven, precariously balancing them on her shoulders. Alex dumps a ladleful of hot malted milk into a cup, which spills over the sides and scalds his hand. "Yeow!" he cries. A waiter announces that Tables 23 and 25 are ready for their desserts right away. Runners gather around our station to whisk off the eight plates of cookies and milk and five apple galettes as soon as Marie plops down scoops of honey ice cream next to the galettes.

Dessert service for the Bar Mitzvah has just begun, later than we anticipated. I thank Alex, the young line cook, for stepping in to help. I roll up my sleeves and get ready to send out about 40 more desserts in quick succession.

Scott the waiter bellows, "Table 30, fire, please!" "Table 30, two cookies and milk, four galettes!" Mariah calls out, and I repeat to confirm, "two cookies and milk, four galettes. Firing!" I quickly pull the soft, warm cookies out of the oven (they are kept warm on a sheet tray at 300°F) with an offset spatula, being careful not to let them fall apart. I slide them onto two plates next to Breton biscuits and cups of warmed malted milk. Marie puts down blackberry compote and sliced almonds on four square plates, then takes the warm galettes out of the oven. When the last galette lands on the plate, I call for runners. Once they're here, I begin scooping ice cream.

Timing is essential when a dessert has contrasting temperatures; you don't want the ice cream to melt, but you don't want the galettes to get cold, either. We are, in this sense, at the mercy of the runners' competence to give our customers desserts in the shape they are intended to be.

Tweny minutes later, we are done. It's a blur. The station is a horrible mess. Now, onto dinner service! We clean up our station, take a quick break, and start all over again.

Today on the list are burger buns (of course), panna cotta, chocolate boxes, huckleberry compote, and sugared pistachios. We are adding the pistachios to the Boca Negra dessert. The original presentation looked a little too bare, and we needed something crunchy to set off the cake's gooey softness.

The burger buns are easy now. I have a better understanding of the nature and character of the dough. I know exactly how the dough should feel when it has been kneaded enough or proofed enough. This is one of those things you just have to practice over and over again until you develop an intuition. I think I finally "get it." As long as the yeast cooperates with me, I probably won't have major issues with the buns from now on.

Panna cotta is an Italian dessert, basically sweetened cream thickened with gelatin. We add mascarpone cheese to ours for extra richness and a vanilla bean for flavor. To make the filling, I whip mascarpone with sugar in the Kitchen Aid until fluffy and light. In a pot, I heat equal parts cream and milk with the vanilla bean (the seeds scraped out), and melt several gelatin sheets (which have been bloomed in cold water) into it. Then I fold the mascarpone-sugar mix into the liquid, and pour the content into individual molds. These take about two hours to set.

The huckleberry compote is also very easy. Place huckleberries in a pot, cover with water, and add sugar to taste with a splash of lemon juice. Cook until the syrup is thickened. This will now accompany the apple galette instead of blackberry compote.

At 5:30 p.m., I take a quick break. I check my phone and find a message from my dear friend, Michelle. She will be visiting from Orange County with two of her friends and will be stopping by G for dessert. I am happy to hear this.

After break I begin to work on the sugared pistachios. This is a technique I learned from Albert. Toast pistachios until slightly brown, about five minutes. Mix sugar with some water (a little more wet than "wet sand" stage), dump in all the nuts, and stir vigorously with a wooden spoon to facilitate crystallization. After about seven minutes, the liquid will evaporate and the syrupy sugar surrounding the nuts will suddenly turn powdery and white. I keep stirring until the nuts are no longer sticky. I pour the nuts out on a sheet tray to cool.

Eric the bartender comes to tell me that Michelle has arrived at the bar. I go out to say hi, then come back to the kitchen to put together a few complimentary dessert plates for her and her two friends. I decide on panna cotta, cookies and milk, and apple galette. They are delighted. Sadly, I only have a few minutes to chat with them. There is still a hefty amount of pre-service prep to do.

The next four hours are a torrential storm of desserts like I've never experienced. Right off the bat an eight-top orders a bunch of doughnuts, so I run over to the fryer, a dozen pieces of brioche dough in hand. When I come back, four minutes later, there are six tickets lined up across the board! Marie helps me set up the plates and informs Jeremy, our general manager, that the desserts will take a few minutes longer than usual.

The rest of the evening proceeds in much the same way. I move as quickly as I can, while trying my best to stay calm inside (like the center of a spinning wheel). My mind has to be clear in order to formulate the most efficient way to get these plates out. This is probably one of the most difficult parts of the job, because there is so much noise and other stimuli assaulting you from all directions. Marie helps me, and somehow we survive this "slam of the century." We are exhilarated, and ready to pass out.

LESSONS/PROBLEMS

When there are more than two sheets of gelatin to bloom, I have to make sure they are separated and submerged in the water side by side (not stacked on top of each other). If they are stuck together, they won't bloom properly and are difficult to melt.

PREDICTIONS

- *Not a busy night*
- *Bake buns*
- *Make Breton dough*

DIARY

It is hot and sunny today. The widget on my laptop screen tells me it is 87 degrees in Los Angeles. The first thing I think of (besides, well, ditching work and going to the beach, in a perfect world) are the chocolate boxes—how hard it is going to be to keep them from getting soft and droopy. We will have to keep them in the bar area for as long as possible.

I will have to construct a few more boxes tonight, but I will wait until later in the evening when the sun has gone down and the temperature inside the kitchen is also cooler.

Instead I decide to work on doughnuts. The brioche dough from yesterday has an overfermented, strong yeast smell, so I toss it in the trash. I take out the new batch of dough made last night, flour the work surface, and tear off a big piece of the wonderfully soft and airy dough that has risen slowly overnight. I roll this out into a flat sheet, and cut out circles. I place the circles on a well-floured sheet tray, cover the tray with plastic, and put it away in the walk-in until service. There is no need to leave the dough out to ferment further this time; I can tell from its soft texture that the yeast has done its thing.

There are a couple of other things I need to make before service: butterscotch cream and Breton dough. These simple tasks, combined, should have taken no more than two hours to complete, but I'm feeling a bit off today.

For the butterscotch cream I use the second recipe Marie and I decided on, after the first one (containing gelatin) proved too unstable. The problem with this one is that it contains a high amount of cornstarch. It burns easily at the bottom of the pot if you're not whisking it constantly and vigorously for the 10 or so minutes it takes to get the milk-starch mixture to come to a boil. Not that I mind it—I sort of enjoy meditative tasks such as this one that calls for my undivided attention.

But all it takes is for me to leave the pot unattended for two minutes, while I walk to the back walk-in to retrieve Plugra butter for the Breton dough. A clump of the blooming cornstarch has stuck to the bottom and burned. Stirring it further would only disperse the blackened, bitter pieces of starch throughout the cream. I think about transferring the unscorched portion of the cream into another pot, but when I taste it I know that it is too late. The burned flavor has already been infused into the batch of cream. It tastes like someone has tossed a fresh cigarette stub into the mixture. Not good.

This leaves me no choice but to start over again. I have enough butterscotch cream in stock to last me through the night, but Marie will need more for Tuesday. Discouraged and tired, I decide to try again after break.

Dinner break turns out to be just the sort of respite I needed. We have spaghetti and meatballs with yellow beet salad. Once we are done eating, Nels, in a particularly jovial mood, suggests we take a "field trip" to the new gourmet ice cream shop a few blocks up the street. We only have reservations for 37 in the books, so there is a little bit of time to spare. So all seven of us pour out the door into the sunlight and enjoy the walk. Our little "girl group" consisting of Leah, another young intern named Sophie, and myself stagger several feet behind the men and giggle at the gang of swaggering boys clad in chef's whites who are hungry for milkshakes.

Nels treats us to strawberry bonbons and malted milkshakes. While waiting for our treats, Leah and I chat with Richard, the store's lead ice cream cook. I think about how Albert had felt insulted by this guy's offer to supply our restaurant with ice cream.

Returning to G, I decide to give the butterscotch cream another try. To shorten the time it takes for the milk-starch mixture to come to a boil (thus lessening the chances of it burning the bottom of the pot), I decide to take half of the milk and heat it together with the caramelized brown sugar and cream. Then I add the cornstarch to the other half, whisk this into the mixture, and cook until thickened. This method works well; I manage to not burn anything. The last step is to add egg yolks. The yolks are tempered with some of the hot liquid before being added to the pot. I cook this for a few more minutes, pour the cream out onto a sheet tray, press plastic wrap directly against the surface to prevent a "skin" from forming, and put it away in the walk-in.

At 8:30 I have not received any dessert orders, and I'm beginning to feel a little tired. I make Breton dough twice, because I forget to add sugar the first time. I put two loaves of brioche in the oven but neglect to take them out, until the wonderful buttery, yeasty aroma turns to the bitter smell of burned toast. To make things worse, the chocolate boxes are wilting. It's just not my night.

Things begin to pick up at 9 p.m. One ticket, two tickets, three... all of a sudden I have six tickets across the board. There are doughnuts to be fried, cookies to be warmed, and sugar-craving people to be fed. No time to feel sorry for myself.

LESSONS/PROBLEMS
The brioche loaves were forgotten in the oven because I had not set the timer (built into the oven) for them. I needed the timer free for use during service. We should buy a freestanding timer. My intuition works most of the time, but not all of the time.

Day 26 *MAY 9*

PREDICTIONS
- *Doughnut night. A very busy one at that*
- *Laurie will be helping me plate*

DIARY

I awake to the news on the radio informing me of a major brush fire that's burning through Griffith Park, threatening L.A. Zoo, the recently renovated Griffith Observatory, and some of the upscale homes in Los Feliz. These homes have been evacuated overnight. Outside the sky is covered in thick, black smoke. My apartment isn't threatened, but I hate the idea that, for the next few days, I will be inhaling all this smoke. And I worry about the animals being driven out of their habitats and wandering the streets. Who will take care of them?

With these thoughts in my mind, I drive to work. It's doughnut night again, but I'm not exactly in the mood to think about doughnuts. But being a professional means to think about doughnuts even when you don't really want to. So I shift my thoughts toward fried dough and its assorted fillings, like I do every Wednesday.

Well, at least Marie makes things a little more interesting for me by giving me a new project to work on. Tonight there will be a small party beginning at 10 p.m. requesting tray-passed hors d'oeuvres and desserts. We are making ginger-infused chocolate truffles. Marie has already tested

GRIFFITH PARK FIRES.

this rather unusual recipe earlier in the day but wants me to make a new batch.

To make gingered truffles, I first melt some dark chocolate in a bowl over simmering water. Then I grate fresh ginger into a small pot of cream, bring it to a boil, and strain the mixture through a cheesecloth-lined chinois (a cone-shaped, fine mesh stainless steel strainer). Being sure that the chocolate and cream are at the same temperature (115 degrees) to avoid breakage, I blend the two together using a hand-held immersion blender. While the blender is running, I add chunks of softened butter until they are incorporated. The result is a rich, smooth ganache with the consistency of old-fashioned chocolate pudding. This will be kept in the refrigerator until hard enough to roll between the hands. Laurie and I finish these off, before the crazy doughnut rush, by dusting them in a mix of ground ginger and cocoa powder.

Next I make the batter for carrot cake doughnuts. I toast walnuts, dissolve yeast in a mixture of crème fraiche and milk, and then whisk in eggs, vanilla and buttermilk. Next, I sift together the dry ingredients in a large bowl (pastry flour, sugar, baking soda and powder, ground ginger, cinnamon, and salt). I make a well in the middle of the dry mix and pour the yeast-liquid mixture into it. Using a spatula, I briskly mix the dough, and all that's left to do is to stir in the walnuts and shredded carrots.

Unbelievably, we are out of carrots. The entire restaurant is out of carrots! Well, plain old carrots do not accompany any of the dishes at G, so running out of carrots isn't a huge threat to the business, but the line cooks do use them to flavor stock. Marie decides to take the matter into her own hands and goes to the nearest market to buy carrots.

In the meantime, I go over the doughnut menu (which hasn't changed from last week) and make sure I have all the necessary fillings and glazes. The Meyer lemon glaze is a bit too loose, so I adjust it by whisking in some powdered sugar. The chocolate pastry cream (for S'mores doughnuts) is still spread on a sheet tray in the back walk-in, so I bring that back and scrape it into a pastry bag. I macerate mixed berries to garnish the plate. Laurie arrives and I quickly review the doughnuts for her.

Thank God she is here, because this turns out to be the most insane doughnut night ever. The ticket printer clatters and spews out tickets nonstop from 8 until 11 p.m. We sell 126 doughnuts all together, many of the tables ordering the All Eight plus three Ice Creams option.

After the last order, the grill cook pops in and says, "Wow, you guys look like you've been hit by a hurricane." Our station is a huge mess of spilled strawberry jam, butterscotch cream chocolate glaze. I look down and my formerly white chef's coat is now as colorful as a tie-dyed t-shirt from Telegraph Avenue in Berkeley.

Laurie says she will help me clean up, but I let her go home. She is volunteering without pay, after all, and she's already helped me a great deal tonight. After cleaning up, I still need to make a big batch of vanilla ice cream base. To mix, stir and thicken the custard (containing 66 egg yolks, separated by hand). To cool it down in an ice bath takes about an hour and a half, and I clock out just before 1 a.m.

LESSONS/PROBLEMS
Don't assume that the savory side has something in stock just because it's a "common" ingredient (i.e., carrots). Whenever we are making something new, we have to make sure we have the necessary ingredients and, if not, order what we need.

Day 27 *MAY 10*

PREDICTIONS

- *Roll and cut Breton cookies*
- *Make brioche*
- *Find out details for party on Saturday*

DIARY

When I walk into the kitchen at 3 p.m., I see a juice blender on our station and recipes for crazy-sounding milkshakes on the clipboard: Siam tea, caramel tequila, and blueberry malt.

Marie has been asked by our press agent to come up with a recipe or two for an unusual beverage, to submit to a magazine doing an article on Los Angeles chefs. We are testing the recipes together and offering samples to our coworkers to determine the best flavor.

Marie made the recipes simple, as they are geared toward the home cook. The blueberry malt calls for vanilla ice cream, blueberries, and malt powder. We blend a batch and pour it into shot glasses for tasting. The consensus is that it is a little too strong on the malt, so we reduce the amount by a tablespoon.

Next, we make Siam tea milkshakes by steeping tea in cream, straining it through a chinois, and blending it with vanilla ice cream. This is delicious and refreshing. Siam tea has an earthy, herbal flavor with hints of mint and citrus.

Caramel tequila is, not surprisingly, everyone's favorite. Marie sneaks off to the bar for a shot of tequila while I prepare the caramel in a small pot (we are adding this to our vanilla ice cream, but the recipe calls for store-bought caramel ice cream). The caramel, ice cream, and tequila are blended together for about ten seconds. Everyone is enthusiastic about this one ("It tastes like butterscotch candy with a kick!" "Wow, this is the best milkshake I've ever had!"). We are a little bit too happy at the conclusion of our successful milkshake recipe test.

There isn't too much to do tonight in terms of pre-service prep. We have only 45 people in the reservation book so far, and we don't want to over-prepare. The only two essential tasks tonight are to roll out and cut Breton dough, and make brioche dough for doughnuts tomorrow.

I quickly take care of the Breton dough, and set up for service. Now we are using squeeze bottles with fine tips, purchased at an art supply store, to dispense the sauces on the plates. Marie insists it's neater and allows for better control than splashing them on with spoons, though I find the spoon method to be more expressive and liberating. I check to see that the three bottles are filled, and place them on top of the oven to warm.

Before Marie leaves, we have a quick discussion of future projects. On Sunday I will begin production for a tasting menu dessert consisting of souffled cheesecake (I like to call it Japanese cheesecake, because this is what you get in Japan if you ask for cheesecake) and wine-glazed Bing cherries.

Cherries are coming into season, finally, and this makes me very happy.

Also on Sunday I will need to come up with a new cookie to replace the Breton on our cookies and milk plate. The Breton biscuits are delicate and delicious, but they are incredibly time-consuming. You have to mix the dough, chill it, roll it out (it's very sticky and temperamental), cut out ovals, eggwash and score the tops, and bake them. I am contemplating something simpler, like a lemon-flavored shortbread.

Between 7 and 9, things are slow. I start gathering the ingredients for my brioche and take an inventory of cookie dough. We are short on chocolate chip, so I make a note of it for Marie to see in the morning. I check my chocolate boxes. A few of them are warped from the heat, curved in the middle and oozing down like Dali's surreal clocks. I quickly salvage the unaffected ones (all four of them!) and put them in a container, taking them to the wine room where it's cool and safe. They will stay there until I need them.

At 9 o'clock I get a sudden flurry of orders. Doughnuts, galette, cookie and milk. It's been a boring night so I'm excited to finally get some action, and I spring toward the deep fryer like a little girl running out to play. I am stopped mid-spring by a loud clash of metal and an acute pain at the base of my right index finger. I let out a shriek and notice that I've rammed my finger into the sharp corner of a hotel pan Anna had placed on top of a garbage bin to hold her sliced red onions. The pan is overturned and the onions are all over the floor now.

"Oh my god, I'm so sorry, Anna!" I bend down to pick up the onions, but she shoos me away, saying, "It's O.K. Worry about your finger, not me, and go finish your desserts."

My finger hurts and I know it's bleeding, but I don't look at it. I have an embarrassing history of fainting from the sight of my own blood. It happened once at the CIA, and once at the Four Seasons. The Four Seasons incident was induced by a tiny little nick on my pinkie that caused a single, pearl-sized droplet of blood to ooze out. My chef called an ambulance, but I came to before it arrived, and felt fine afterward.

Not wanting to bring about another humiliating scene, I quickly cover my right hand with a latex glove and continue working. Clumsily I pipe the cream into the doughnuts, spilling half of it on the counter, and I ask the waiter picking up the plate to scoop the brown sugar ice cream for me because my hand can't handle the pressure at the moment.

When the counter is clear, I pull the glove off. There are two neat half-inch incisions near the knuckle, forming an arrow pointing toward the fingertip. The corner of the pan has imprinted itself onto my hand. There is blood, but it's not so bad, and I manage not to pass out. What's ugly is the flesh underneath the broken skin; it's bruised and purple.

After the accident, there are still three tables waiting for desserts. Now the sensation is more like a dull muscle ache than the sharp, stabbing pain it was upon impact. I manage to finish my job with a little help from the waiters (who are bored by this time, anyway, waiting for the lingering customers to polish off their bottomless glasses of wine).

LESSONS/PROBLEMS

Even though my job is endlessly fascinating, sometimes it's smart not to get too excited. This ugly scar on my finger is proof.

FRESH LAVENDER FOR MY NEW COOKIES.

Day 28 *MAY 11*

PREDICTIONS

- *Busy night (118 people in the book as of Thursday night)*
- *Assemble galettes*
- *Janet coming to help me plate*

DIARY

After a good workout at the gym, I feel calm and energized as I arrive at work today. This serves me well, as Fridays are always busy and require a high degree of mental focus. Tonight there will be a party of 15 panna cotta or apple galettes, so my first task is to assemble the galettes.

LAVENDER-CHAMOMILE SHORTBREAD

I take out the frozen puff pastry circles, and while they thaw I check the ice cream freezer to be sure we have enough of each flavor. Marie has spun two containers of honey for the galettes. I check all the flavors for taste and consistency. Everything seems good.

Marie mentions that the butterscotch cream filling for doughnuts made last week has a grainy texture. I taste this too, and understand what she means. It is not obvious, but if you put a small amount of it in your mouth and run your tongue against the roof of the mouth, you can feel tiny solid particles interrupting the creaminess. I suspect it's curdled egg. Maybe I wasn't whisking fast enough when tempering the yolks with the hot cream/sugar mixture. Maybe I forgot to strain the custard before it set up.

Next time, we will try a new method (hopefully this will be the last one!). We will make a similar custard base containing cream, milk, egg yolks and brown sugar but, instead of adding cold eggs to hot liquid, everything will be mixed together cold. The resulting mixture will be poured into half-hotel pans set over full hotel pans with hot water in them. These will be covered with foil and baked at a low temperature until the custard is thickened. This is the same method used to make crème brulée, which has a satiny, flawless texture if made correctly.

I set up my station as usual, and show Janet how to assemble the galettes. In the meantime, I decide to work on a new cookie. We are running low on the Breton, so I can't wait until Sunday. I try to think of a cookie that's "refined" enough to replace the Breton biscuits. The other two, chocolate chip and ginger, are homey drop-style cookies, so the third has to be different. What's buttery, pretty, and easy to make? Shortbread! I'm going to do shortbread. But plain old shortbread would be unimpressive. So I decide to infuse some lavender-chamomile tea into the dough, by melting the butter and steeping the tea in it until its flavor is pronounced. I also add a few stems of beautiful, vibrant fresh lavender, which Marie had picked up at the market on Wednesday. The cookies turn out surprisingly good. Since we have so much fresh lavender, I'm also storing some in an air-tight container with sugar to make lavender sugar. This will be dusted on the edges of the cookies before baking. My new baby, the lavender-chamomile shortbread, will go "official" on the menu tomorrow. I'm excited.

At 5:30 p.m., we take a break. For the staff meal tonight: socca galette, bamboo rice, arugula salad. It's a healthy and delicious meal. Socca galette is a savory pancake made with chickpeas. Bamboo rice is short-grain white rice infused with the chlorophyll of bamboo, giving it a grassy color and Vitamin B. Arugula salad is just that—baby arugula leaves dressed with apple cider vinaigrette. Every once in a while we have exotic stuff like this, depending on the whim of the line cooks in charge or what's left over from service.

It's a busy night. We end up doing 128 covers (about 40percent order dessert). The best sellers of the night are, unpredictably, panna cotta and lemon meringue. We usually sell two or three, definitely not more than five of each per night, but tonight they are so popular I completely run out of panna cotta and have just two lemon meringue left. Weird. These fruity desserts are likely to be popular with mothers, too, so we will need to make a lot more for Mother's Day on Sunday.

Janet stays until the end and helps me clean up. She asks if she can come and volunteer again on Sunday. I tell her yes, and she does a little celebratory dance. At midnight I clock out. Not a bad night.

LESSONS/PROBLEMS

The melted butter infused with lavender takes a long time to come back together. First I refrigerate it. Thirty minutes later, it's still pure liquid. I put it in the ice cream freezer. Still doesn't do much. Out of desperation I think of this: put the bowl of melted butter over another bowl filled with ice, and whisk it. This works well. The butter is solidifying before my eyes and, in about five minutes, it is ready to be beaten with powdered sugar.

*A GIFT FROM MARIE: BING CHERRIES,
PINOT NOIR.*

Day 29 *MAY 13*

PREDICTIONS
- *Busy night: Mother's Day*
- *Work on next week's tasting menu*

DIARY

Mother's Day 2007 begins with happy news of a new mother. When I call my mother to pay my respects, she tells me that my older brother and his wife (who are successful artists living in Tokyo) are expecting a baby. I will be an aunt for the first time. We plan to join them in Japan early next year to celebrate the birth.

The thought puts a spring in my step and I look forward to going to work, even though it's not going to be a typically mellow Sunday night. Tonight we are expecting about 100 guests. Marie has the night off, as usual, but she will be bringing her mother to the restaurant later for desserts.

When I arrive, I find a lovely display of fresh Bing cherries and a bottle of domestic Pinot Noir gracing my station, with a note from Marie. She has been to the market with her mother, and picked these up for me, remembering that I am planning on a new tasting menu dessert consisting of souffled cheesecake and wine-glazed cherries. This is very sweet of her.

Janet, the former flight attendant, is back to help me get through service. She is doing this on her own accord, without pay, and Nels is unlikely to hire her due to lack of experience. Soon, Marie will have to tell her the truth, so that she will not waste any more of her time waiting for us to make an offer. But tonight, she is having a blast, shaping cookie dough and shamelessly flirting with all our waiters, and we're in a position where we can really use an extra hand, so why spoil it?

While she helps me with station setup, I begin to reduce the Pinot Noir with some sugar in a small pot. After about an hour, this will reach the consistency of maple syrup. The sauce will be spooned over souffled cheesecake.

Souffled cheesecake, or Japanese cheesecake as I like to call it, is one of my favorite things to make (and eat) in the world. It's about as similar to super-dense, sickeningly rich New York-style cheesecake as a hummingbird is to a domesticated turkey that can't fly. The texture is light as air when the cake passes through your lips, but turns creamy once you sink your teeth into the pillowy softness. The flavor is delicate, a little tangy, and not too sweet.

What makes it so light, as evident from the name, is the soufflé method. Eggs are separated and the whites whipped to stiff peaks. The yolks are mixed in with cream cheese, sugar, a tiny bit of cornstarch, and vanilla extract. The whites are folded in gently at the end, being careful not to deflate them.

Further contributing to the unique texture of Japanese cheesecake is its baking method. The batter is poured into greased and floured pans, and the pans are placed in a hotel pan filled with hot water. Certain custards, such as crème brulée, are similarly baked in a water bath. This facilitates a steam-filled oven, helping the cake to retain moisture.

The cherries will be pitted, cut in half, and dressed with the Pinot Noir sauce to order. They will be served on top of the cheesecake.

After a meal break at 5:00, we go through the last steps of pre-service prep. The earliest tables are seated at 6:45, and there are many of them. We get our first order around 7:30 p.m., and from there it's non-stop plating. Janet assists me by frying doughnuts, heating up milk for the cookie plate, and keeping things organized and clean around our station. That is, when she's not flirting with the waiters or telling me stories about her mid-air flirtations with customers at her old airline job. I will certainly miss her company.

Marie arrives at the bar in a pretty black dress (instead of her usual ensemble of loose pants, white cotton jacket, and hair secured with a pink bandana; it's always illuminating to see our coworkers in non-work mode for the first time), accompanying her mother, around 10 p.m. We send out a succession of desserts, not stopping until the waiter lets us know when they've had their fill. We end up serving every dessert on the menu, adding two scoops of her favorite caramelized chocolate ice cream to conclude the extravaganza.

The two deliriously happy women come into the kitchen to thank us. We are just closing up and our station is a disorganized mess. Marie asks us how service went, and Janet proudly tells her not to worry about a thing, everything went well and the tasting menu is ready for next week. Her mother seems very pleased. Marie and I exchange our favorite lines from "Love and Death" once again, making each other laugh idiotically.

Even though I didn't get to spend time with my own mom (she moved out of state with our dad and two adorable dogs a year ago), Mother's Day was filled with simple, happy moments. I have my job to thank for this.

LESSONS/PROBLEMS
When baking the souffled cheesecake, I lined the square

pans with parchment paper on the bottom and up the sides. One corner of the paper fell into the batter (probably blown by the oven fan) and baked right into it. Next time I will trim the paper so that there's not so much overhang.

EVERYBODY NEEDS DOWNTIME: FOUNTAIN AT THE HUNTINGTON GARDENS.

Day 30 *MAY 20*

PREDICTIONS

- *Discuss new milkshake project with Marie*
- *Train new girl on burger buns*

DIARY

Writing about my work has been grounding, revealing, frustrating, and therapeutic all at once. Once you get in the habit of transcribing your life onto paper, you become more mindful of what happens around you, and painfully aware of your strengths and weaknesses. When I started this diary, I never imagined so much could happen in the course of 30 days.

Today I have a new boss, new duties, a new schedule, a new assistant to train, several new coworkers, a triangle scar on my right hand, and a renewed sense of gratitude for a job I love and am still passionate about.

After Janet, two other aspiring pastry chefs volunteered with us. We hired Elaine, a recent culinary school graduate and a former nurse, to take over plating three nights a week. This means I will have three days of production, two nights of plating, and Sundays (and Mondays, because we are closed) off! This is unprecedented in the history of my employment in the culinary field.

I am now busy training Elaine on station setup, plating and closing the station. She is extremely attentive, quick, and has the ability to remain calm under pressure, qualities which were probably required of her as a nurse and a mother of three. We are very happy to have her. Now there are three women in the pastry department, and the line cooks (mostly male) regard us as a sort of warm, inviting oasis of fresh-baked cookies and encouraging spirits amid the machismo and rowdiness of the main kitchen.

Han and I still struggle with our schedule differences, and have not seen much of each other lately. We are both concentrating on our careers. At least that's the excuse we keep giving each other. It really is a challenge to be in a functional relationship when you work in the restaurant business and your partner doesn't. But now that I have Sundays off, we are hoping to make it work. Remember: nothing is permanent. Everything changes eventually.

The restaurant business, and the culinary field as a whole, is truly dynamic. There will be ups and downs, burned fingers and emotional breakdowns, people coming and going, an endless creative process that might make you feel ecstatic one day and despondent the next. No two days are the same.

It takes a strong mind and body, and above all, commitment to persevere in this field, but the rewards are many. Working in a kitchen stimulates all of your senses. There's always something sweet and buttery in the oven, filling up the air with instant aromatherapy. There's always something to taste, whether it's a new crop of nectarines from the market or fried zucchini blossoms the line cook presses you to try with a touch of sea salt on top. There is just as much to see (intense glowing purple of huckleberries), feel (smooth, elastic brioche dough) and hear (people, clanking metals, running water), every day, all the time.

Working with fresh ingredients from the farmer's market makes me feel connected to the earth and its changing seasons (which are not obvious if you live in Southern California). There is no job that makes me feel more alive.

Because of this constant assault to the senses as well as the vibrant energy of my coworkers, my job is highly absorbing. I think of work not as drudgery but a healthy escape from life's mundane problems.

The truly great thing about my job, however, is that I can live pretty much anywhere I want, and not worry about finding a job. In every city in every part of the world, people need to eat. Since finishing school in 2002, I've worked in four major cities in the U.S, on the East Coast and the West Coast, and a few spots in between. Wherever you go, you will find this great little community of chefs who will embrace you, as long as your drive is genuine.

This is my last Sunday shift. I am not dressing burger buns with egg wash and sesame seeds, or sweet-talking them into rising. I am not working alone, either. We are all here: Marie, Elaine, me.

I have trained Elaine on the burger buns, since she will be taking over from next Sunday on. Marie is here because she is demonstrating her new pet project to us. The idea is: Doughnut Nights are so popular, so how about Milkshake Nights on Sundays, to accompany the burgers? With five different flavors, and five different toppings?

I turn to Elaine with a mocking smile, nodding emphatically. "Good Lord," she mutters, as she lifts the sheet tray of beautifully proofed buns and slides it into the oven.

OTHER CAREER DIARIES

Career Diary of an Animation Producer
Sue Riedl
ISBN: 1-58965-011-5

Career Diary of an Animation Studio Owner
Joseph Daniels
ISBN: 1-58965-010-7

Career Diary of a Caterer
Jennifer Heigl
ISBN: 1-58965-031-X

Career Diary of a Composer
Patrick Smith
ISBN: 1-58965-024-7

Career Diary of a Dental Hygienist
Nancy Aulie
ISBN: 1-58965-042-5

Career Diary of a Marketing Director
Christa Bahr
ISBN: 1-58965-045-X

Career Diary of a Newspaper Reporter
Hamil R. Harris
ISBN: 1-58965-033-6

Career Diary of a Publication Design Director
Leon Lawrence III
ISBN: 1-58965-030-1

Career Diary of a Social Worker
Diana R. Hoover
ISBN: 1-58965-034-4

Career Diary of a Teacher
Carol Anderson
ISBN: 1-58965-035-2

Career Diary of a TV Production Manager
Craig Thornton
ISBN: 1-58965-015-8

Career Diary of a TV Show Host
Author: Hilary Kennedy
ISBN: 1-58965-044-1

Career Diary of a Veterinarian
Christine D. Calder
ISBN: 1-58965-043-3

Career Diary of a Vocalist
Nikki Rich
ISBN: 1-58965-037-9

Career Diary of a Web Designer
C. R. Bell
ISBN: 1-58965-022-0

Available at bookstores everywhere. For more information on these and other titles in the Gardner's Guide Series, visit www.GoGardner. com.